THE
PIED
PIPER

ENOCH BURKE

THE
PIED
PIPER

Is John Piper and New Calvinism Destroying the Church?

Burke
Publishing

THE PIED PIPER
PUBLISHED BY BURKE PUBLISHING
Cloonsunna, Castlebar
Co. Mayo, F23 W625
Ireland

Scripture quotations taken from the Authorized Version of the Holy Bible.

Printed in the United Kingdom
Third Printing, 2018
ISBN 978-1-9999355-0-4

Cover design by Josiah E. Burke
Cover image used with permission
The author has made every effort to ensure the accuracy of the information within this book was correct at time of publication.

FOR PURCHASES AND ORDERING, WRITE TO:
BURKE PUBLISHING
Cloonsunna, Castlebar
Co. Mayo, F23 W625
Ireland

For permissions contact: info@thepiedpiperbook.com or visit http://www.
thepiedpiperbook.com

Contents

Let us build with you.

EZRA 4:2

Introduction

*...It was needful for me to write unto you, and
exhort you that ye should earnestly contend for the
faith which was once delivered unto the saints.*

JUDE 3

E arlier this year I stood at the foot of the famous Martyrs'
Memorial monument just outside Balliol College in Oxford.
A family member was completing studies in Oxford at the
time and had invited me over to visit. I had some time to linger in
the streets of this ancient city and wanted to prioritise becoming
acquainted with anything of spiritual worth.

The monument is imposing, situated at a pivotal point
overlooking a busy junction. It commemorates three men (Hugh
Latimer, Nicholas Ridley and Thomas Cranmer) who died for
their faith, being burned in nearby Broad Street. The inscription
on the monument records that they "near this spot yielded their

bodies to be burned, bearing witness to the sacred truths which they had affirmed and maintained against the errors of the Church of Rome, and rejoicing that to them it was given not only to believe in Christ, but also to suffer for His sake."

> To them it was given not only to believe in Christ, but also to suffer for His sake.

Hugh Latimer's words have often rang in my ears, when engaged in my own battles against those opposed to truth. I am thinking of the words he spoke to his fellow martyr as death drew near: "Play the man Ridley; we shall this day light such a fire in England as shall never be put out."[1]

A few yards up the road from this great monument lies another venue of historical significance. It is a public house, or an inn as the English sometimes call it, called "The Eagle and the Child." It is famed as the location where British academic C.S. Lewis spent many hours discussing spiritual subjects over alcoholic beverages.

I can think of many differences between Lewis and Latimer, the martyr whose blood was spilled only yards from where Lewis drank. Those I will list in a moment. Two similarities, even only two, however, spring to mind: both men claimed to follow Christ, and both men inspired others to follow in their steps.

The fire which Latimer prophesied did indeed sweep England. Within 50 years of his death, England was a Protestant nation, and today it continues to enjoy an academic and cultural heritage stemming from his vision.

C.S. Lewis, on the other hand, has inspired a different cohort of people. When Lewis drank in the Eagle and the Child, England was still overwhelmingly Protestant; today, however, this is no longer the case. This must, in part, be ascribed to factors which Lewis aided and supported: Lewis was an Anglo-Catholic who never professed to be an evangelical, believed in purgatory, and regularly went to Roman confession. He married a divorcee and combined frequent discussion of spiritual topics with a dissolute life. Sadly, much of English Christendom has followed in his steps.

If there is one person who has propagandised C.S. Lewis to professing Christians today, it is John Piper. Piper is well known around the world as a leader in Christian teaching. He has written over 50 books, spoken at hundreds of conferences, and caused thousands to follow his ministry.

> If there is one person who has propagandised C.S. Lewis to professing Christians today, it is John Piper.

Piper has never hidden his core beliefs. He is a hedonist who believes that God created man to be happy. His message contradicts the clear teachings of Scripture, as well as the testimony of thousands who have lived and died for the faith.

Piper's message is not new. There have been heretics in the past who preached similar messages. What is different about Piper is the packaging on the poison. Piper was brought up in a professedly fundamentalist Christian home and he has garnered a wide following amongst younger fundamentalists. Indeed, it could be argued that much of Piper's popularity has occurred at the expense of fundamentalist churches.

During my late teens, I experienced the call of God into the ministry at a Bible conference. Shortly afterwards, I applied to a seminary not far from where I lived but was rejected because of my conservative views on marriage and divorce. Following this, I enrolled in the North American Reformed Seminary, an online seminary which offered a curriculum drawn from a variety of sources.

Over the next few years, I encountered New Calvinism and gradually came to imbibe some of its tenets. I was encouraged to question all of the traditional Christian beliefs which I had been instructed in by my parents from my youth. I became more comfortable around ungodly people, and felt that it was my duty to become more engaged in their social pursuits. On one occasion, I had signed up for a recreational and social activity in my part-time workplace, and was called into the office by the manager. He informed me that the social part of the outing would be taking place in a bar, and that he wanted to let me know as he didn't feel it would sit with my religious convictions. I felt ashamed that it had taken an ungodly man to call attention to the incongruity of a believer desiring to attend such a function.

In God's providence, it took several factors to cause me to see the error of my judgment and to return to a historic understanding of God, salvation and sanctification; most important, however, was the discipline of a godly mother and father. Without them, I doubt (except for the goodness of God) that I would have changed course. They firmly pointed out to me the error of my ways, the destruction that attended compromise and worldliness, and the disconnect between the superficiality of New Calvinist ideas and the simplicity that is in Christ Jesus. I came back to the Lord, but, for a long time, false ideas from this period of backsliding still lingered in my mind.

New Calvinism and the philosophy of John Piper, "Christian" hedonism, has made great inroads into the church, especially amongst young people of my generation. It is my prayer and hope that this book will expose its charade of lies, warn unsuspecting souls and "contend for the faith once delivered to the saints."

Enoch Burke

Jeremiah 23:28-29

Castlebar, Ireland

November 2017

I can do no other.

MARTIN LUTHER

1 | Why John Piper?

Beloved, believe not every spirit, but try the spirits whether they are of God: because many false prophets are gone out into the world.

1 JOHN 4:1

The last 35 years have seen the Christian church change dramatically. By "Christian" I mean those who profess salvation through Christ alone, by faith alone. Today there is almost no line of separation between the Christian and the world, far less emphasis on traditional missions and outreach, and little knowledge of what the Scripture says on the issues of our day.

In the last 35 years there has also been a dramatic increase in the influence of one man, John Piper, and a concurrent rise (a little later) of a movement largely inspired by him: New Calvinism.

Piper was born in 1946; by the late 1990s his books had sold over a quarter of a million volumes. His subsequent rise to a commanding leadership of much of evangelicalism could be described as meteoric, and he has been described by fellow New Calvinists as the Reformed "rock star".[2]

In 1980, Piper became pastor of Bethlehem Baptist Church in Minneapolis, Minnesota. Since then, he has written over 50 books, started Desiring God ministries (the 9th most popular Christian website in the world), and opened, with his church, a new college and seminary. His influence stretches throughout the USA and around the world. Piper often speaks at conferences, including the annual Passion Conference in Atlanta, Georgia which has an estimated 50,000 young people in attendance. Piper also travels around the globe: in 2010, for example, he was a featured speaker at the Third Lausanne Congress on World Evangelisation in Cape Town Africa.[3]

Piper retired from the pastorate of Bethlehem Baptist Church in Minnesota in 2013 after 33 years leading the church. During his tenure, the church grew to become a multi-campus church in downtown Minneapolis with thousands of congregants. The initial growth of the church in the 1980s has been credited to the attendance of young people whom Piper influenced while lecturer at Bethel Seminary in Minnesota (20 minutes' drive from Bethlehem Baptist). Shortly after his arriving at the church, Piper

> John Piper has been described by fellow New Calvinists as the Reformed "rock star".

declared "it is time for us at Bethlehem to clarify and make explicit our commitment to Christian Hedonism" (1983).

It appears that much of the growth at Bethlehem Baptist Church was due to the establishment of the church on the new ideas of Piper rather than the normal pattern of church growth through traditional evangelism. David Mathis, one of Piper's co-workers at Bethlehem declares: "One of the first things I learned after arriving at Bethlehem in the fall of 2003 was that 'Pastor John' was not nearly as celebrated in Minneapolis as 'Piper' was in parts of the Bible Belt. He seemed relatively unknown in the Twin Cities, and his South Minneapolis neighbourhood was largely unaware it had an author in its midst so well known in other parts of the country."[4]

Mathis' comments suggest that Piper's following was predominantly from those who had encountered Piper through his writing rather than his evangelistic efforts.

Piper became well-known on the evangelical scene in 1986 after the publishing of his book Desiring God. This popularized a core belief of John Piper's which he describes as Christian Hedonism. This novel belief gained in popularity in the first decade of the 21st century with the rapid growth of New Calvinism, a relatively recent movement which galvanised in the early 2000s and infamously mingles historic doctrines of the Reformation with many modern culture trends.

The explosion of New Calvinism in the church has been hailed as a great boon to the church by many. They point to the attendance of younger people at churches, the multitude of new books being published, and the international flavour of the movement's appeal.

Many pastors and leaders, however, see in the movement anything but a work of God. They have watched its development with dismay, but have kept largely silent. They have seen God and His truth not "desired" but denigrated. They have watched as the youth which they nurtured in the faith forsook their counsel, and often their churches, for a new and socially acceptable Christianity. They have seen an influx of worldliness into the church, everything from tattoos to consumption of alcohol and dancing. Most of all, true pastors have witnessed a loss of reverence for the God that they love, and have seen genuine piety and spirituality decline and not increase.

A Background in Fundamentalism

Piper grew up in a home which professed to be fundamentalist. He is the son of the late Bill and Ruth Piper, missionaries who had strong links with fundamentalist Bob Jones (Bill Piper was a trustee at Bob Jones College (BJC) for some time). Notably, however, even in those early days Piper's parents were questioning of the militant stance which fundamentalism adopted against compromise. In June 1957, Bill Piper resigned from the board of BJC after raising questions around the school's condemnation of Billy Graham's ecumenical crusade in New York. Bill Piper later sought to distinguish between what he termed the (undesirable) "attitude" and the (desirable) "doctrine" of fundamentalism.

[5] In 1957, Billy Graham held a crusade in New York from May 15 to September 1 in which a reputed 2 million people, cumulatively, were in attendance.[6] The crusade marked a major break in Graham's career, however, as it was the first time in which

10

he openly cooperated with modernists on a large scale. The crusade was held in response to an invitation from the Protestant Council of New York, and Graham organised the campaign in cooperation with churches participating in the National and World Council of Churches. This placed him firmly at odds with fundamentalists, who believed him to be (as Bob Jones Sr. stated), peddling a "discount type of religion" and "sacrificing the cause of evangelism on the altar of temporary convenience".[7] Graham responded forcefully by declaring that he would "preach the gospel anywhere" (an argument which is still regularly made by his progeny today): "I intend to go anywhere, sponsored by anybody, to preach the gospel of Christ, if there are no strings attached to my message. ... The one badge of Christian discipleship is not orthodoxy but love. Christians are not limited to any church. The only question is: are you committed to Christ?"[8]

> The New York Crusade was the first time Billy Graham openly cooperated with modernists on a large scale.

Bill Piper clearly took the side of Billy Graham in this matter, even though Graham was in open collaboration with those who denied the gospel. It was quickly proven that fundamentalist' concern with Graham had been well-founded. As far back as 1950, the Roman Catholic Archbishop Cushing (later a cardinal) of Boston had endorsed a Billy Graham crusade, and after 1957 Graham began to collaborate with Roman Catholics in organising his crusades, treating them as representatives of the Christian faith. Graham went on to meet Pope John Paul II no fewer than 3 times, and proudly relayed that the pope had said to him in private, "we are brothers."[9] It is not surprising that John Piper has also proved to be extremely duplicitous on the issue of the Roman Catholic Church, especially on its status, and that of its members, in the eyes of God. Little surprise, when his father championed the cause of Billy Graham when John Piper was barely 10 years old.

It is said that "heresy, by its very nature, cannot peacefully co-exist with the truth."[10] John Piper has built his whole ministry on convincing thousands that they can embrace the fundamental doctrines of truth while eschewing any attitude that would draw the ire of the world. Thus, he has divided families and churches once unified in their stand for truth.

> It is said that "heresy, by its very nature, cannot peacefully co-exist with the truth."

New Calvinism presents itself as "new". In general, its most prominent ambassadors are those in the neo-evangelical tradition. What is notable, however, is that New Calvinism has enamoured many in the Fundamentalist or Old School Evangelical circles. Indeed, New Calvinist leaders appear to go out of their way in targeting Fundamentalists and convincing them (especially the younger generations) to reconsider their identity and change their beliefs on some of the most fundamental issues of Christianity. Most importantly, they have succeeded in convincing large swathes of the church that it is possible to hold to the doctrines of the Faith while having a "joyful attitude", i.e. giving no offence to a world that hates God and opposes His truth.

12

Truth: Absolute and Unchanging

In contrast to the New Calvinists of today, all the New Testament writers framed their inspired account of the Truth, as something which looked back to and built upon the testimony of the Old Testament prophets, not something new. Peter declared that what he wrote was the same "salvation the prophets have inquired and searched diligently" (1 Peter 1:10). Jude contended for the "faith which was once delivered unto the saints" (Jude 3).

Moses, while giving the second reading of the law of God to the new generation of Israelites, prefaced it with a solemn warning: "Ye shall not add unto the word which I command you, neither shall ye diminish ought from it, that ye may keep the commandment" (Deut. 4:2). Special caution was to be exercised to ensure that the Word of God was neither altered nor changed: nothing was to be added to it or taken from it. This is not the only occasion where this warning was issued; it appears again in Deuteronomy 12:32. The Galatians were found guilty by Paul of removing themselves "from him that called you into the grace of Christ unto another gospel" and roundly rebuked (Gal. 1:6). Migration to a different gospel is a threat which faced the church as vividly in the first century as it does today. Thus, the commendation which Paul had for Timothy was that, from his childhood, he had "known the holy scriptures" and he urged him to "continue in the things which thou hast learned" (2 Tim. 3:14-15).

Today it is popular for pulpit and pew to profess their love for truth; it is far less popular, however, to contend for it. The word contend found in Jude 1:3 ("ye should earnestly contend for the faith"), comes from the Latin word contendere which means "to strive." To be valiant for the truth is to defend it, to assert it, to maintain it (Jer. 9:3). The more earnestly the truth is opposed, and the more men pervert the right ways of the Lord, then the more God's people must not only love the truth but contend for it. Jude did not merely command to contend for the faith but exhorted the believers to earnestly contend, pouring their energies into this holy task. Yes, those who contend for the faith will doubtlessly be labelled contentious, but we must leave the consequences to God (Neh. 6:3-7; Gal. 2:11-14).

The final qualification of an elder which Paul mentions to Titus is that he be found "holding fast the faithful word as he hath been taught" (Titus 1:9). Paul valued the teaching which men and women received, and believed that what was taught should be prized and retained for future generations. In times of error such as the present, many false teachers lead young minds astray by encouraging them to slight what they have been taught by their parents and their churches and to "discover" new truths for themselves. This approach is wholly unscriptural and the pole opposite to the approach which Paul fosters in Scripture.

From cover to cover, the Scripture promotes and values order, discipline, faithfulness and instruction. Truth is absolute and unchanging, and should be faithfully taught, and passed on from one generation to the next (2 Tim. 1:5). The writer of Hebrews, faced with the task of defending Christianity against those who called new converts back to Judaism, commanded his readers to "give the more earnest heed to the things which we have heard" and reminded them of the great salvation which "at the first began to be spoken by the Lord" (Hebrews 2:1-3).

14

Heresy, Heretics and Infiltration

Times of heresy are challenging times. Nevertheless, if the church stands by the truth and exposes the heretic, they can be times of great revival. Why? The Apostle Paul sets forth the reason in 1 Corinthians 11:19: "For there must be also heresies among you, that they which are approved may be made manifest among you." Paul was writing to a church where many in the congregation had separated themselves into different sects, much like the current craze after the worldliness of New Calvinism. He argued that the division had come, however, so that the approval of God on those who stayed faithful would become evident. Amid gross error, God's truth would become stronger than ever by the testimony of those who remained faithful to it.

Heresy, according to the Merriam-Webster dictionary is "adherence to a religious opinion contrary to church dogma."[11] The beliefs of the Christian church since the Reformation (and beforehand) have often been codified in catechism format. The beliefs which Piper has promoted, especially his core doctrine of "Christian" hedonism, mark a clear departure from this historic faith. Piper, as an adherent and proponent of such beliefs is, I believe, a heretic.

> The Apostle Paul argued that heresies had come so that the approval of God on those who stayed faithful would become evident.

There is no shortage of biblical passages that warn of heretics' proclivity to infiltrate the church.

Jude's first prerogative was to demonstrate that infiltration had a historical precedent (Jude 5-7): in the Exodus, amongst the angels of heaven, and in the cities of the early inhabitants of Canaan. The book of Ezra records the first desire of the "adversaries of Judah and Benjamin" as being to infiltrate the work: "let us build with you: for we seek your God, as ye do; and we do sacrifice unto Him" (Ezra 4:2). Paul notes that even in the early days of his ministry in Jerusalem, false brethren had crept in unawares to "spy out our liberty which we have in Christ Jesus" (Gal. 2:4). Peter prophesied that the early church would surely experience "false teachers... who privily shall bring in damnable heresies" (2 Pet. 2:1).

False teachers varnish over their message with a veneer to deceive the unsuspecting and give the appearance of orthodoxy. They are experts in manifesting plausible pretences, in order that the church might unawares take heresy into its bosom. They "lie in wait to deceive" (Eph. 4:14). They "beguile" (to deprive by trickery) the unsuspecting of their spiritual wealth (Col. 2:18). Christ warned of them as being as spiritually dangerous as ravenous wolves in the guise of a sheep (Mt. 7:15).

A heretic must offer an unsuspecting church something more than what it already has. Usually, whether directly or indirectly, he offers it a greater liberty, a greater license to sin. Marcion (2nd century), one of the earliest of heretics, rejected the Old Testament in its entirety. Few heretics today are as overt in their antinomianism, yet they are antinomian no less. Peter warned that the false teachers would "allure through the lusts of the flesh" (2 Pet. 2:18). Their appeal attracts the foolish and unlearned: "the simple believeth every word" (Pr. 14:15). The beguiled are those who, rather than making full use of their senses, refuse to weigh

16

the words and the life of the false teacher against the truth of God's word (Heb. 5:14; 1 Jn. 4:1; 1 Thess. 5:21).

The Church's Duty to the Truth

The church's duty towards the truth is twofold. It has a mandate to proclaim God's word to the present generation and it is a trustee to keep and preserve that truth for generations to come. It is charged to profess the truth and endure martyrdom, if necessary, in its role as the "pillar and ground of the truth" (1 Tim. 3:15).

Each believer has a responsibility in this great task. To preserve truth is to present it pure to the next generation. As the Ark of the Covenant served to preserve a copy of the law of God, so the church serves as a guardian of the truth (Deut. 31:26). God's Word serves as a witness against the church if it strays from it, just as the law in the Ark served the same purpose: "that it may be there for a witness against thee" (Deut. 31:26). The true believer makes the cause of truth his own, embraces this responsibility, and rejoices in the "glorious gospel of the blessed God...committed to my trust" (1 Tim. 1:11).

One of the greatest strengths of the unadulterated gospel is its simplicity. Christ did not preach a complicated message (Mt. 11:28-30; Mk. 1:15). The Apostle to the Gentiles rejoiced in the simplicity of the message which he carried, and regarded complication of it as certain corruption: "I fear, lest by any means, as the serpent beguiled Eve through his subtilty, so your minds should be corrupted from the simplicity that is in Christ" (2 Cor. 11:3). He summarised the gospel which he preached as equally accessible to both Jew and Gentile: "repentance toward God and faith toward our Lord Jesus Christ" (Acts 20:21).

The glorious message of the gospel is freedom from sin (Mt. 1:21), a truth bound up with the very name of the Messiah. Those saved have no leave to sin; rather, they have a liberty to serve God (1 Jn. 3:8). They have been freed from the slavish service they once made to the devil and sin. Paul

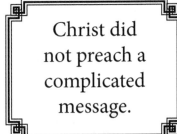

Christ did not preach a complicated message.

rejects soundly the argument that salvation by faith ushers in a carelessness about sin (Rom. 6:1). The gospel grasped becomes a teacher to the Christian, exhorting him or her to "deny ungodliness and worldly lusts" (Titus 2:12). The grace of God is an incentive to holiness, not pleasure in sin (Rom. 6:16), and an aid to purity (2 Cor. 7:1).

This book argues that New Calvinism is not the authentic gospel but a departure from the "faith which was once delivered to the saints" (Jude 1:3). Furthermore, John Piper is the "emperor with no clothes on" that is leading this movement. Piper is especially popular with young people,[12] a generation that is easily excited, theologically illiterate and extremely impressionable. The development of digital technology has magnified Piper's impact, and he has made full use of such, including social media, to spread his message; at the time of writing he has almost 1 million followers on Twitter. How tragic if the church today would fail in its obligation to leave to its posterity a clear and faithful account of the demands of God and the true gospel (Ps. 44:1).

What follows is a short account of the fruit of Piper's doctrine and belief system in his own life, and the marked departures from the Christian faith which Piper has introduced and popularised in the church.

The propagators of error… have thus always put themselves in strong contrast with the true "messengers" of Christ, whose office is to deliver to the world a simple testimony, nothing more, nothing less.

JAMES B. RAMSEY

2 | The Real John Piper

*That we henceforth be no more children, tossed
to and fro, and carried about with every wind
of doctrine, by the sleight of men, and cunning
craftiness, whereby they lie in weight to deceive.*

EPHESIANS 4:14

J ohn Piper's doctrine can be summarised in one simple
statement: you can have both. You can have holiness and levity.
You can have pleasure and God. You can have the world and

the church.

I remember that as a child I often had a poor record of discerning the real from the counterfeit. This became an especially unfortunate trait to have as popular use of the internet soared in the mid-2000s. When I was in my early teens, I was unable to resist the allure of technology, especially the new camera phones of the day. On one occasion, I gave £20 of my hard-earned money to buy a place in a pyramid-style scheme which promised me a phone worth hundreds of pounds. I dutifully posted the money to the address on the website, but never heard anything of the promised phone (or my money!) in the aftermath.

Discernment and common sense, I quickly learned, can save you lots of time and money.

Scripture calls every Christian to discernment, and to be "no more children...carried about with every wind of doctrine" (Eph. 4:14). Foolishness is something we associate with children, the ignorant and the immature. Naivety in material matters can cost you a lot (as I learned), but naivety in spiritual matters will cost you far more. Hence Paul warned the young church at Ephesus of the "sleight of men, and cunning craftiness, whereby they lie in wait to deceive." Sleight here means "craft or cunning employed so as to deceive"[13] and interestingly, Paul warned that it would come in terms of "winds" of doctrine, which, having no root in God's word, were heretical. These heretics would draw the foolish away from the truth.

The only answer to heresy is to know the truth so well (Eph. 4:15) that one becomes spiritually mature, fit to readily identify and expose error. There is only one way to know the truth and that is to be a student of sacred Scripture, guided by the quickening of the Holy Spirit. In a day when error is spreading far and wide, the need to be established in the truth (2 Pet. 1:12) is greater than ever. False doctrines are without truth or solidity, and do not lend themselves to the establishing of the saint.

John Piper's Hedonism

Piper terms his cardinal doctrine Christian Hedonism, the core belief of his life which he came to in the late 1960s. This belief, which he defines as "God is most glorified in us when we are most satisfied in Him"[14] was not prompted by a study of the Scriptures. Rather, it was inspired by his reading of three men: the Roman Catholic philosopher Blaise Pascal, the Anglo-Catholic C. S. Lewis and the neo-evangelical Daniel Fuller who rejects the inerrancy of the Scripture.

Piper's hedonism is not just a doctrine; rather, it is a belief system which reduces the glorious gospel of the everlasting God to a psychological notion which occurs in the recesses of the mind. His doctrine is a cultic philosophy which adds to the basic tenets of the faith (Pr. 30:6), and redefines Christian definitions of sin, salvation, sanctification, and the character of God. The core argument of "Christian" hedonism, that God is glorified by a hedonistic approach to life, is never once found in Scripture. Rather, it is an invention of Piper to draw followers to himself and a departure from the simplicity of the Scripture.

James Ramsey, the 19th century expositor, commented powerfully in his commentary on Revelation regarding false teachers and their doctrines. I reproduce here his faithful analysis of the methods of false teachers:

> Ever since the times...of those false teachers of Corinth, who withstood Paul with their professions of superior wisdom, the defenders and propagators of error have laid claim to deeper insight and profounder views. They are ever boasting of a progressive theology, a system more rational and in harmony with nature, of certain profoundities of reason, which are only depths of Satanic deception...they have thus always put themselves in strong contrast with the true "messengers" of Christ, whose office is to deliver to the world a simple testimony, nothing more, nothing less.[15]

Piper's "Christian Hedonism" claims to offer a "deeper insight" into the experience of knowing God, but its new doctrines amount to a departure from thousands of years of true interpretation of the Scriptures. His hedonism appears more "profound" than the "faith once delivered to the saints" but it is that very "profundity" that betrays it as something new and something heretical. It is this "boasting of a more progressive theology" that betrays a marked departure from the "simple testimony" which the church has heretofore delivered to a lost and dying world.

> The core argument of 'Christian' hedonism, that God is glorified by a hedonistic approach to life, is never once found in Scripture.

24

John Piper's Antinomianism

The fruit of Piper's doctrine is antinomianism; that is, a belief that the Christian does not have to keep the law to please God. Piper does not believe that Adam and Eve's first sin was primarily a breaking of God's commandment.[16] Neither does he believe that those reconciled to God are blessed by their devotion to God in keeping His commandments. Furthermore, Piper's gospel does not emphasise repentance, where sinners turn from breaking God's law to obeying it.

By contrast, the salvation which the Scripture speaks of always results in a changed life. James spoke of a gospel devoid of repentance when he declared that "faith, if it hath not works, is dead, being alone" (James 2:17). Obviously, there were hedonists who claimed to be Christians in his day also. A profession of faith, if found alone, does not save, and is of no consequence. Rather, true faith is never alone, but is evidenced by

> Piper does not believe that Adam and Eve's first sin was primarily a breaking of God's commandment.

works, works which will commend it on the day of judgment: "And I saw the dead, small and great, stand before God; and the books were opened: and another book was opened, which is the book of life: and the dead were judged out of those things which were written in the books, according to their works" (Rev 20:12). The only faith in James which is alone is the faith of devils (James 2:19): it is a bare mental assent, devoid of any spiritual benefit. It is not sufficient to save, for faith without works is dead.

Against the spectre of antinomianism, James raises the testimony of two Old Testament saints: Abraham and Rahab. Both had a living faith. Abraham's faith produced good works and endeared him to God (Gen. 22:16-17; James 2:21-23). His living faith granted him peculiar favours and intimacies with God. The Scripture is thus clear that to have Abraham's blessing we must have his faith, an evidential faith.

James adduces the selflessness of Rahab as further proof that living faith is seen, not heard. Rahab had lived as a harlot, but had discarded her former way of life, and come to fear Jehovah. Five verses of Scripture record her words of faith (Josh. 2:9-13), but it is her actions that verified

> The only faith in James which is alone is the faith of devils.

the nature of her faith. Her encounter with the messengers and her identification with their welfare, at great risk to her own life, proved her faith to be genuine: "was not Rahab the harlot justified by works, when she had received the messengers, and had sent them out another way?" (James 2:25)

Saving faith, in Scripture, always expresses itself in actions. The three Hebrew children were defined by their visible, external refusal to break God's commandments and bow to the image which the egoistical king had made (Daniel 3:18). Almighty God had said regarding the making of and obeisance to images: "Thou shalt not bow down thyself to them" (Ex. 20:5). These Hebrews trusted and obeyed God rather than man, resolving to die in their integrity rather than compromise in any form. Commandment-keeping was their forte and God honoured them with glorious confirmation of His approval and His presence. Were their faith a psychological mind-game they would have quickly been lost in the fawning crowd.

Down throughout the history of the church, men and women have been defined by their allegiance to God's truth. Foxe's Book of Martyrs accounts of servants of God who died for something greater than themselves. John Foxe, born in 1517 in Lincolnshire, tells the story of the many valiant servants of God, male and female, some in their teens, others in their nineties, who suffered martyrdom for their unrelenting allegiance to the truths of Scripture: Patrick Hamilton, Jane Grey, John Hooper and many more. Of Hooper it was said that he spent "three quarters of an hour or more in the fire."[17] These were not hedonists in any sense of the word. To reduce God's calling to such a term is a satanic assault on the grace of God and an unvarnished attempt to hoodwink God's elect.

Piper's false gospel sits very well with the spirit of our age and the assault on God in the public sphere. The atheistic movement for a secular state in countries once renowned for their acknowledgement of God is more than satisfied if believers "have their faith but keep it to themselves." This sits well with Piper's doctrine, which emphasises self-centredness and empty emotion rather than selfless action, and has crippled the church from carrying Christ's demands into the public square.

Piper's doctrine has led to a decline in common-sense Christianity in action when it comes to the political sphere. When an important amendment protecting marriage was put to public vote in the state of Minnesota in 2012 (Piper's church is located in Minneapolis, the largest city in Minnesota), the local Star Tribune

27

reported that John Piper was not going to advise his congregants (numbering in the thousands) how to vote. A spokesperson for him stated: "He [Piper] wants to avoid the political realm as much as possible. The Christian Gospel is not left, it's not right."[18]

Here Piper evidences, by his heretical departure from true Christian works, that he is no more concerned for the glory of God than the devils who believe.

John Piper in Historical Context

Neo-evangelicalism as a movement began in the late 1940s in the USA in opposition to the militancy and biblical separatism of fundamentalism. It was characterised by a new emphasis on dialogue and by its non-judgmental attitude. One of its leading lights, Harold J. Ockenga, wrote in 1976 that neo-evangelicalism "while reaffirming the theological view of fundamentalism, ...repudiated its ecclesiology and its social theory."[19]

Throughout the second half of the 20th century, neo-evangelicalism and fundamentalism went separate ways, with the former becoming mired in controversy surrounding issues such as ecumenism (Billy Graham's cooperation with Roman Catholics was central here) and inerrancy.

Piper is a neo-evangelical, both in belief and in practise. He claims that while listening to the neo-evangelical leader Ockenga speak on radio in 1965 while in Wheaton College, he was called to the ministry. In contrast to other neo-evangelicals of his generation, however, Piper has garnered a large following in fundamentalist circles. He claims that he has been greatly influenced by "fundamentalist, conservative evangelical, progressive evangelical, and Reformed sources."[20]

What few realise, however, is that John Piper is not fundamentalist in his doctrine in any practical sense of the word. Rather, Piper's feet are firmly in the neo-evangelical camp. A decade or so after his father left the board of Bob Jones College (later Bob Jones University), Piper enrolled in the neo-evangelical school Wheaton College in Illinois. Later Piper enrolled in a Master of Divinity (MDiv) program at Fuller Theological Seminary in Pasadena, California, as well as the University of Munich in Germany, where he published a thesis entitled "Love your Enemies."

Wheaton College is a Protestant liberal arts college in Illinois in the USA. Its most famous graduate is Billy Graham. John Piper attended Wheaton College at a time (mid-1960s) when it had moved away from fundamentalism to a more ecumenical approach. The president of Wheaton when Piper enrolled in 1964, V. Raymond Edman, was a spiritual father to Billy Graham and was elected Senior Vice President of the Billy Graham Evangelistic Association in 1965. Prior to Edman's appointment, Wheaton College had fired J. Oliver Buswell from the role. Buswell was a Presbyterian renowned for his staunch Calvinism and fundamentalist separatism from the apostasy of his day.

Fuller Theological Seminary, where Piper studied from 1968 to 1971, was firmly aligned with the neo-evangelical camp which firmly opposed the separatist element of fundamentalism. Fuller Seminary, under the leadership of Daniel Fuller, dropped its belief in the Scriptures being "free from all error in the whole and in the part" from its doctrinal statement in 1972 in a rejection of inerrancy. Notwithstanding, John Piper says in his most popular book Desiring God (2011 edition): "I remain ever in debt to Daniel Fuller in all I do. It was in his class in 1968 that the seminal discoveries were made."[21]

John Piper's education has been one which schooled him in neo-evangelical techniques of appeasement, compromise and dialogue. His greatest achievement is that so few examine his doctrine or the effects of his teaching, but rather accept his professions of orthodoxy at face value.

> Piper's greatest achievement is that so few examine his doctrine or the effects of his teaching, but rather accept his professions of orthodoxy at face value.

Following his graduation from the University of Munich, Piper taught at Bethel Seminary in St. Paul, Minnesota, before leaving academia for the pastorate in 1980. Bethel Seminary, however, later employed Greg Boyd, who subsequently became the leading advocate of open theism (a doctrinal system which opposes the foreknowledge of God, and stresses God's love instead).

Piper's flagship website, Desiring God, contains many articles which deal overtly with Fundamentalism. Unlike the Neo-Evangelicals of the 1960s, however, Piper does not criticise Fundamentalists. Rather, he insidiously commends them and thus steals their hearts. In one of his articles, published in 2008 and titled "20 Reasons I Don't Take Potshots at Fundamentalists",

Piper flatters Fundamentalists with lines such as "they tend to raise law- abiding, chaste children" and "they resist trendiness" despite the fact that his own life belies his flattery on both counts.[22]

✗   Piper has spawned a movement, however, which has been very successful in undermining what fundamentalists stood for and thinning its ranks. Many are enamoured by what he says and do not take the time to examine the life of the man, the testimony of his family, and the content and origin of his beliefs. The Scripture says in Proverbs 20:11 "even a child is known by his doings, whether his work be pure, and whether it be right." A closer examination of Piper's own family, and the legacy which he leaves in those closest to him, gives us a greater insight into this man whose influence has grown out of bounds in Christian circles.

John Piper's Family

John Piper married Noël in 1968 and has four sons (Karsten Luke, Benjamin, Abraham, and Barnabas) and one adopted daughter (Talitha).

Noël Piper

Noël also studied at Wheaton College: it was while studying there in 1966 she met John Piper. The two married in 1968.

Noël has written books, but not as many as her husband. One of the most substantial books which she has written is entitled Treasuring God in Our Traditions which was published in 2003 by Crossway Books. The book emphasises the importance of traditions handed down from one generation to another.

In 2009, the Pipers posted a Christmas message video[23] from their home to the Desiring God website. In the video, Noël declares "if you come to our house the first thing you would notice is manger scenes everywhere." The manger scenes can be seen in the video as Noël speaks. Noël continues to say that "scattered all around [our house] are other manger scenes because we like to remind ourselves that Jesus is the Saviour of the world." Such crib scenes, of course, are a staple in Roman Catholic households, depicting as they do the Son of God in a statue format.

Noël does not mention the Word of God in her video message. It is important to be reminded of the words of Christ, who warned His disciples to be on guard against traditions, lest they take the place of the commandments of God: "in vain do they worship me...laying aside the commandment of God, ye hold the tradition of men" (Mark 7:7-9). Christ rebuked the scribes and Pharisees, saying, "why do ye also transgress the commandment of God by your tradition" (Mt. 15:3) and exposing their use of tradition to empty God's Word of its power: "Thus have ye made the commandment of God of none effect by your tradition" (Mt. 15:6).

Talitha Piper

Talitha Ruth Piper was adopted by the Pipers in 1996. She is now 22. Talitha works at Passion City Church, located in Atlanta, Georgia. Passion Church is led by Louie Giglio, who also organises the annual Passion Conferences where tens of thousands of young people rave to loud music under strobe lights.

In October 2017, Talitha listed Ed Sheeran as one of her "top four favourite artists to listen to currently" and also stated "My favourite movies from the past year: Wonder Woman, You've Got Mail (finally watched it!), all the Harry Potter movies (also finally watched)."[24] Ed Sheeran is renowned for regularly wrapping himself in the LGBTQ pride flag to climax the end of his live sell-out concerts. The Harry Potter movies and books, meanwhile, glorify elements of astrology, divination, numerology, and clairvoyance, all features of real world occultism.

Piper's beliefs are further reflected in his sons; two of them, Barnabas and Abraham, have commented widely on their beliefs via public media and have discussed the influence of their beliefs on their personal lives. Like many New Calvinists, their lives show little evidence of true salvation: Abraham Piper founded and manages a multi-million-dollar entertainment blog while his brother Barnabas is a divorcee whose widely publicised views on marriage reflect a departure from Christian faith and practice.

Abraham Piper

It is common knowledge that Abraham Piper for many years lived a life of drunkenness and immorality, at a time when his father was pastor of Bethlehem Baptist Church. John Piper did not resign from the ministry, despite the disrepute his son's actions were bringing to the church.

In 2007, Abraham wrote a widely-published article for the Billy Graham Evangelical Association's Decision Magazine detailing his supposed return to Christianity, and counselling Christian parents on how to "reach out to your wayward child."[25] He advises Christian families whose children are living in gross sin that the child's sin is not the real problem, but rather that they "don't see Jesus clearly." His article is laced with anti-scriptural psychology, including advising parents that their children don't "need pointed out that what they're doing is wrong" and that while rebuke might be necessary, "you're probably not the one to tell them."[26] His advice is in conflict with the sentiment of Scripture on child-rearing: God commended the Abraham of Scripture, for example, saying, "For I know him, that he will command his children and his household after him, and they shall keep the way of the LORD, to do justice and judgment" (Gen. 18:19).

Abraham Piper currently lives in Los Angeles and runs a digital media company called Brain Jolt Media.[27] His twitter feed (as well as his profile description) includes occurrences of profanity. One of his main projects is a blog he founded entitled 22 words which made $17m in profit in 2016. In August 2014, 22 words produced a blasphemous video clip entitled "Jesus takes the Ice Bucket Challenge" which garnered thousands of views and is still liked by Abraham Piper on his public profile.[28]

> Abraham Piper's advice is in conflict with the sentiment of Scripture on child-rearing.

The clip makes a mockery of the taking of God's name in vain and parodies the atonement. It is a creation which would be inconceivable for any true believer to produce or endorse, and constitutes a crystal-clear case of blasphemy.

Barnabas Piper

Piper's youngest son, Barnabas Piper, has published three books and works for Lifeway, a Christian book publisher in the USA. He has two daughters and currently resides in Nashville.

> Piper's beliefs have not inculcated in his children a deep love for truth and chastity of life.

Barnabas Piper is no closer to orthodoxy than his father. An interview with him broadcast by David C. Cook in 2015 gives Barnabas' advice on getting a tattoo. He states that for him, a tattoo is "something that is meaningful to me, ... kind of like tying a string around your finger to remind you of something."[29] Barnabas tattooed a verse onto his body, just before his 30th birthday, when he declares he was "a few years after coming through a really rough time."

Barnabas Piper announced his divorce in early 2017. Although claiming to be a Christian, Barnabas immediately went public with his divorce, in a move uncharacteristic of a believer. He published a blog post declaring that his marriage of over 11 years had died, having been "dying for a long time,"[30] language which does not mirror a scriptural understanding of the inviolability of the marriage bond. Barnabas, despite having two daughters from the marriage, declared that he had decided to stop praying for his wife and was "moving on,"[31] disagreeing that he should pursue reconciliation. He continues to publish and speak in a leadership role.[32]

Piper's beliefs have not inculcated in his children a deep love for truth and chastity of life. Rather, his children espouse teachings which are just as heretical as those of their father. There is little reverence for God or respect for historic Christian doctrine on relationships and holiness of life.

In past generations, and indeed in the pages of Scripture, we find that a man was measured as much if not more by the life which he lived as by the profession which he professed. Charles Bridges, the magnificent expositor of the 19th century English church, declares in his commentary on Proverbs: "The discussion of the substance of religion without reverence, without a sense of the Divine presence, and a single eye to edification, is only a profanation of holy things, and at best must alienate the precious truths from their true purpose."33 Bridges understood that the edification of the hearer was the only valid goal of spiritual discussion, and that discussion without such a goal was a negative exercise which would devalue the very truth it claimed to advance.

> "The discussion of the substance of religion without reverence...is only a profanation of holy things, and at best must alienate the precious truths from their true purpose."

Piper has popularised a doctrine, "Christian" hedonism, which claims to exalt God and His salvation but wholly undermines the great calling of God to "walk in the light" (1 Jn. 1:7). The unbalanced hedonism of Piper's theology profanes the

36

grace of God, which teaches the saint rather to "deny ungodliness and worldly lusts…[and] live soberly, righteously and godly, in this present world" (Titus 2:12). The impact of Piper's teaching upon his followers is a practical antinomianism, and this is the one real test of his teaching. This is the real John Piper, when one looks beyond the books, the popularity, and the great sweeping statements calculated to impress. When Piper comes, therefore, claiming new insight into the truths of Scripture, the church should see him for what he really is. All the evidence suggests that this spirit is not of God (1 Jn. 4:1).

The law of God expresses the mind of the Creator.

Arthur W. Pink

3 | The Doctrine of John Piper

I fear…your minds should be corrupted from the simplicity that is in Christ.

2 CORINTHIANS 11:3

Somehow, doctrinal equivocation is the new avant-garde of our day. Doctrinal accuracy is welcomed, but only if it concerns what we agree or disagree on inside our heads (what we believe). Once clarification is sought regarding the rest of our bodies (Christian practice), however, caution is exhorted, compromise is welcomed, and confusion is the result.

During my time at the National University of Ireland Galway, I was elected Chairperson of the Christian Union for 2013 and 2014. Prior to that, the Union met in the Roman Catholic chapel. Public events were few and the major points of contention which divide the Christian from the world were not addressed. Sexual sin and consumption of alcohol destroy many students of the university, yet there was no clear sound on these issues emanating from the Christian Union and its leadership. Indeed, there was very little contention for the faith, and it was customary instead for professing Christians to make their way to the public house after the weekly meeting had finished. This was all, I might add, under the auspices of the International Fellowship of Evangelical Students (IFES). The Christianity exhibited had become a reflection of the doctrine espoused: insular, fuzzy, irrelevant. Even the University's Societies Officer referred to them as "namby-pamby" and much of their outreach to the campus seemed to be serving tea and coffee to the unregenerate.

Similar to IFES, the New Calvinist movement exhibits an interest in doctrine which often does not promote a robust, healthy, godly approach to Christian living. The New Calvinist movement majors on doctrinal considerations, but these are often of the "heads" type. John Piper's website Desiring God is one of the Top 10 most popular "Christian" websites on the internet.[34] It contains thousands of articles, videos and sound clips. Much of this teaching, however, is devoid of the delicate balance between word and walk which has characterised truly spiritual ministries. Furthermore, as we will see, there is a clear pattern of new emphases in John Piper's teaching which sets it apart from the doctrine espoused by men of God in church history past.

Is Preaching the Gospel Enough?

The peculiarity of the New Calvinist movement, and John Piper especially, is its focus on "the Gospel." New Calvinists are continually talking about the gospel. Every day of the week sees new blog posts written on this subject, and every month new books are published. Authors and bloggers talk about the glory of the gospel, the centrality of the gospel, the effects of the gospel. Every part of life is viewed through "gospel lenses". Sinners are counselled, the church-going are exhorted, and the lost are evangelized all through effusive speech on the merit of the gospel.

Any objective observer can see, however, that this framework marks a departure from the balance of subjects treated in Christianity of bygone days. The gospel was indeed preached, but it was done so in a scriptural fashion, where sinners were exhorted to repent, and the saints urged to edify themselves and contend for the faith (see Jude 1:3 and 1:20). No New Testament writer preaches Christ divorced from repentance and discipleship. No God-breathed text treats of salvation without also mentioning sanctification. All of Scripture exhibits a glorious and delicate balance, "that the man of God may be perfect (or complete), throughly furnished unto all good works" (2 Tim. 3:17).

Supplanting God's Word with Psychology

Paul, writing to the Corinthians, defended himself against the allegations of false teachers by expressing his own concerns: "I fear...[that] your minds should be corrupted from the simplicity that is in Christ" (2 Cor. 11:3). Paul here warns the Corinthians

41

that their minds could become corrupted, using the Greek word phtheiro which means to "destroy, corrupt or ruin." The same word is used by John in Revelation where he speaks of the corruption of the earth by fornication (Rev. 19:2), and also by Jude in his epistle on false teachers (Jude 10).

If something becomes corrupted, it becomes, in many cases, irretrievably damaged. A corrupted "hard-drive," for example, can cost thousands to repair, if repair is even an option. Interestingly, Paul warns that corruption in the Christian mind would evidence itself in a departure from the "simplicity that is in Christ." The advance of heresy, Paul warned, would be accompanied by a complication of doctrine which would deviate from the pure testimony of Scripture and corrupt the hearers.

A departure from traditional Christian admonition is prominent in Piper's writings. This is especially clear in situations where direct instruction is called for. In a recent post, penned in response to an enquiry from a professing Christian who confessed gross sexual sin (adultery and prostitution), Piper states: "open your eyes, open your eyes as you look at God's crystal-clear word, God's crystal clear gospel, God's crystal clear warnings, God's crystal clear promises that are 10,000 times more precious than any sexual escapade."[35] In this article, written in February 2016, Piper mentions "see" or "seeing" ten times, but "obedience" only once, focussing

> The focus of Piper's writing is not calling sin as sin, or providing simple instruction to forsake the sin mentioned.

rather on a new "understanding" which Piper claims will help this man.

It is impossible to align Piper's response in this situation to similar situations from the pages of Scripture. When Christ encountered the woman taken in adultery, He admonished her to "go, and sin no more" (John 8:11). These were the last recorded words which He spoke to her. The clarity and brevity of Christ's words to this woman are to be observed, as they were a feature of His ministry. To the impotent man of John 5, Christ gave a similar instruction: "Behold, thou art made whole: sin no more, lest a worse thing come unto thee" (John 5:14).

To the unsuspecting, Piper's words may seem like good advice. On closer inspection, however, the focus of his writing is not calling sin as sin, or providing simple instruction to forsake the sin mentioned. Piper's response runs to over 1300 words, but he only mentions sin three times (and two of those are restatements of the question posed). There is a subjectivity to Piper's language which circumvents the clarity of God's word and instead preoccupies itself with the psychology of the sinner.

This sentimentality in exhortation is typical of New Calvinist writers. Piper mentions the word "helpless" ten times, with a focus on the man seeing himself as not helpless but empowered. He speaks about "putting on glasses" and "seeing reality" but there is little engagement with the Scriptural pronouncements on lust and the severity with which God's word approaches sexual sin. A close examination of Piper and other New Calvinists' writings reveals that their emphases are not the same as those of godly evangelical writers in the 18th, 19th and early 20th centuries.

Bringing the Church on a Road Back to Rome

In many respects, New Calvinism has, in its call to Christians to *Wow* "see" new things in the Gospel, more in common with Roman Catholicism than true, biblical Protestantism. Ever since the Reformation, when the focus was returned to the written Word and simple obedience to its clear precepts, Rome has fought back. Its mission is to undermine the simplicity of biblical Christianity by enveloping it in tradition, mysticism and heresy, and it works steadily to undermine those who valiantly proclaim God's truth.

> John Piper's emphasis upon an imaginary holiness, as well as his ecumenical emphasis upon dialogue and discussion, has placed him in opposition to the authority of God's Word.

John Piper's emphasis upon an imaginary holiness, as well as his ecumenical emphasis upon dialogue and discussion, has placed him in opposition to the authority of God's Word. This ecumenical approach is clear in Piper's close relationship with men such as the populist author Rick Warren. Piper conducted an interview lasting 98 minutes with Rick Warren at Warren's Saddleback Church on 1 May 2011, expressly stating as his motive: "My aim in this interview is to bring out and clarify what Rick Warren believes about these biblical doctrines...in doing this my hope is that the thousands of pastors and lay people who look to Rick for inspiration and wisdom will see the profound place that doctrine has in his mind and heart."[36] The same Rick Warren, in November 2014, was a guest speaker at a colloquium at the Vatican, where he urged Protestants to join with Pope Francis in a support of common goals, declaring: "If you love Jesus, we're on the same team."[37] Warren's slavish subservience to the Vatican was seen when he quipped in a later interview, responding to a question as to why he attended the colloquium: "when the Pope invites you, you go."[38]

Sad!

Rome argues against the perspicuity of the Scriptures, that is, the ability of the ordinary man or woman to understand for themselves and by themselves what God has written. The Reformation made the extra-biblical office of the priest redundant, and birthed a generation of independent expositors of the Bible. Rome, by contrast, trains its priests to instruct the people, advocates the use of images and statues to educate the ignorant, and keeps the masses dependent upon its blasphemous services.

Similar to Rome, New Calvinists have failed to develop in their followers a deep love for and knowledge of the Word of God. *True* Rather, they have perpetuated a whole stream of publishing, with every new book promising better, fresher insight than the one before. Just like the priests and bishops of Rome, New Calvinist leaders have developed hagiographical status, with men such as

> Rome argues against the perspicuity of the Scriptures, that is, the ability of the ordinary man or woman to understand for themselves and by themselves what God has written.

John Piper, Tim Keller and Mark Driscoll cultivating a huge (and unhealthy) following amongst young people whose lives show no evidence of a genuine fear of God. Furthermore, the books of these men are often theological topic studies rather than biblical theology or biblical exposition. A partial list of John Piper's works is provided in the table shown as an illustration: many of Piper's works consist of prolonged arguments on behalf of his doctrine of "Christian Hedonism", with the doctrine approached from a variety of standpoints.

Year	Title
1986	Desiring God: Meditations of a Christian Hedonist
1991	The Pleasures of God
2001	Seeing and Savouring Jesus Christ
2001	The Dangerous Duty of Delight: Daring to Make God the Object of Your Desire
2004	When I Don't Desire God: How to Fight for Joy
2005	Sex and the Supremacy of Christ
2006	Taste and See: Savouring the Supremacy of God in All of Life
2007	Battling Unbelief: Defeating Sin with Superior Pleasure
2010	A Sweet and Bitter Providence: Sex, Race and the Sovereignty of God

Beyond all his other writings, Piper's book *Living by Faith in Future Grace* has been especially criticised by theologians as paying lip service to Reformed doctrines but subtly emphasizing salvation by one's personal fulfilment of the "covenant of grace".[39] Piper claims to accept Biblical soteriology; his book, however, first published in 1995, challenges the commonly accepted definitions of works, merit, grace and faith. Piper approvingly quotes Daniel Fuller's comment that "a faith that only looks back to Christ's death and resurrection is not sufficient."[40]

Writing in 2002, the late John W. Robbins of The Trinity Foundation noted that Piper offered no examination in the book of Christ's perfect obedience to God, or Adam and Christ as our legal representatives (see Romans 5).[41]

Robbins suggests that Piper's approach is part of a wider "rediscovery of the Roman Catholic doctrine of salvation."[42]

John Piper has a much closer relationship with the Roman Catholic Church than may at first appear: in an article written in 2003 he approvingly quotes Richard Neuhaus, an evangelical Lutheran pastor who famously converted to Catholicism in 1990.[43]

As far back as 1981, Piper described Mother Teresa as the "tireless old Catholic servant of God" thus conveying his belief that Mother Teresa was an exemplary, hard-working, servant of Christ while simultaneously being a fully subscribed member of the Roman Catholic apostate church.[44]

Mother Teresa, as is common knowledge, was known worldwide as a devout Roman Catholic nun who was fully devoted to the false doctrines of Rome. Piper's comments on the Roman Catholic Church have regularly included "smokescreens": in 2013 he referred to the Pope as a "teacher of the church" and affirmed that "God is willing to save us even when our grasp of the gospel may be partial or defective."[45]

Sad

Whenever Piper even appears to criticise the Roman Catholic apostate system, his words and statements are usually so measured that the effect of any censure is quickly lost. This is a far cry from the clarity and authority (1 Cor. 14:8) of the Reformers and the martyrs down through the centuries who died for their defence of the gospel in opposition to the darkness of the Roman system. The second martyr of the Scottish Reformation, David Stratton, martyred in 1534, exhorted those assembled to "lay aside their superstitious and idolatrous notions, and employ their time in seeking the true light of the Gospel."[46] Compared with such valiant men, Piper's refusal to vigorously oppose a system which presents error as truth and deceives billions is a fault which cannot be overlooked.

In December 2009, Piper was asked in an interview, "If you had two minutes to talk with the pope, what would you say to him?" Piper answered that the content of his conversation would be theology: the doctrine of justification by faith alone. He said that if the pope refused to accept this definition of justification, he (Piper) would say: ""I think that right at the core of Roman Catholic theology is a heresy," or something like that."[47]

> Piper's refusal to vigorously oppose a system which presents error as truth and deceives billions is a fault which cannot be overlooked.

A few years later, however, Piper appeared to row back somewhat on even this very weak and watery rebuke of Rome. In March 2013, he posted an article at Desiring God entitled "Clarifying My Words About Roman Catholic 'Heresy'" and stating "heresy is a strong word... I think it is possible to inconsistently deny the truth of imputation while embracing other aspects of the gospel (blood bought forgiveness, and propitiation, for example), through which God mercifully saves."[48] Piper went on to state, "I am thankful that God is willing to save us even when our grasp of the gospel may be partial or defective. None of us has a comprehensive or perfect grasp of it." In other words, Piper made sure that any offense which might have been caused by his initial comment was completely explained away.

Piper's vacillation on this question can be compared with what Billy Graham said when he was asked what would he say if the Pope invited him to preach at St. Peter's Basilica in the Vatican City: "I would gladly and humbly accept...[and] study for about a year in preparing."[49] Graham was eager to build a bridge to Roman Catholicism and stated that, other than papal infallibility, "there was not much else about which he and believing Catholics differed."[50]

Both Piper and Graham's fundamental approach to Rome can be expressed as follows: a very uncertain sound (1 Cor. 14:8). With Graham, Rome is so close to the truth and errs so slightly from the gospel that you would need to study your Bible deeply to know what to say to correct them. In Piper's case, to huffle and puffle and giggle and then eventually say that you think that "at the heart of the Roman Catholic church is a heresy or something" is too harsh an approach to take, with too much danger of being misunderstood. If a believer was looking to Piper for the correct approach to employ towards Romanists, they would be justified in thinking that they'd perhaps be better not to say anything at all.

Losing Balance by Incomplete Exegesis

The message of New Calvinism is often betrayed by what it does not contain more than by what it does. Writings of New Calvinists do not reflect the full counsel of God's Word when it comes to repentance, the new creature in Christ Jesus, obedience, and the importance of God's law. Piper and his followers speak far more about the Gospel (out of context) than even the New Testament writers, and far less about obedience, reverence and the fear of God.

New Calvinists' teaching is not well-rounded; rather, its imbalance leads souls astray. They preach the privileges of the Gospel before its duties. They preach the love of God before His wrath and His fear. While Piper professes to hold to the Scriptures as the Word of God, his exegesis of Scripture does not reflect historic Christian interpretation, nor the character of God as historically embraced by true believers.

Even less evidence of the Scriptures' teaching or the character of God is seen in the adherents of Piper's new ideas, who are largely ignorant of God's law, dismissive of historic Christian practices and indistinguishable from the world. Piper's followers are likely to emphasize grace over law, love over obedience, and forgiveness over faithfulness, disregarding the careful balance of the Scriptures. This imbalance and opposition to scriptural truth is clearest in the daily life of New Calvinists: convictions regarding separation from the world, consumption of alcohol, standards of dress, purity of life, and abstinence from dancing, pubbing and sexual immorality are soon forgotten.

> The adherents of Piper's new ideas are largely ignorant of God's law, dismissive of historic Christian practices and indistinguishable from the world.

Tragically, the world and the cults can often see this quicker than the church. In the Roman Catholic periodical *First Things*,[51] a recent article on consumption of alcohol in community and the tradition of monks producing liquor ended with the quip: "Who knows? Perhaps even some of John Piper's Christian hedonists will join us there in fellowship, reflection, and friendly dialogue on the witness of these saints."[52]

An Adversion to the Law of God

There is no doubt that the current age is one where lawlessness abounds. Christ prophesied the coming of such an age in His Olivet discourse: "And because iniquity (*or lawlessness*) shall abound, the love of many shall wax cold" (Mt. 24:12). The lawlessness that abounded, Christ warned, would adversely affect the spiritual temperature of many, and lead to a decline in spiritual sensibilities. It is significant that Christ here presented lawlessness and love as inversely proportional: the increase of one was accompanied by the demise of the other.

51

Over 100 years ago, the expositor Arthur W. Pink stated that "the supreme test of love is the desire to please the one loved."[53] Pink entertained no sentimental definitions of love: from a close reading of Scripture he believed that love to God could only be expressed by "conformity to His known wishes" and "obedience to His will." Pink was immersed in the Scriptures, and traced the spiritual decline of his time to the rise of a superficial Christianity. Such Christianity, according to Pink, was spurious, because it failed to fulfil the test of true love for God (and hence, true regeneration) as revealed in the Scriptures: "He that hath My commandments, and keepeth them, he it is that loveth Me" (Jn. 14:21). Pink viewed the popular devaluing of obedience by the pulpiteers of his day as a sign of a defunct Christianity and heretical imposters in the ministry. To the true Christian, Pink emphasised (as the Apostle John had), "His commandments are not grievous" (1 John 5:3).

John Piper has made no secret of his disregard for the law of God. When asked in an interview in 2010, "Are Christians under the 10 commandments?", Piper answered: "No. The Bible says we're not under the law."[54] Piper goes on to elaborate on his statement, but he has made clear where his heart lies. Later in the interview, John Piper's denigration of the law of God is evident when he says in response to 1 John 5:3, "That brings us back to the question, which commandments? I would say, the ones that are loving." A statement such as this amounts to a pick-and-mix Christianity which sits in judgment upon God's law and accommodates the rebellion against authority which is the trademark of the age.

The law of God is a rule of life for the Christian, not in order to be saved (Jesus Christ has perfectly fulfilled the law in our stead), but as a standard for moral conduct. The saints in all ages have taken great delight in following God's law (Psalm 1, Psalm 119 and Rom. 7.22). The Christian has a great heritage to emulate, knowing that obedience to the commands of God is the proof of our love to Christ and our delight in the new nature.

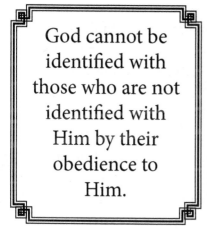

God cannot be identified with those who are not identified with Him by their obedience to Him.

The Apostle Paul, contrasting the righteousness from God which justifies the sinner with the righteousness of the law which guides the sanctification of the saint, quotes at two key junctures the Old Testament words "the man that doeth them shall live in them": Romans 10:5 and Galatians 3:12. In both places, Paul was contrasting the form and purpose of the law with faith. Often overlooked is the fact that Paul saw encapsulated in Leviticus 18:5 a summary of the purpose and glory of the law. The moral law then, and still now, exalts the one who keeps it with a proper motive, not to be justified before God, but to please Him: "Ye shall therefore keep my statutes, and my judgments: which if a man do, he shall live in them: I am the LORD" (Lev. 18:5).

Made abundantly clear throughout the book of Leviticus is the simple truth that God cannot be identified with those who are not identified with Him, i.e. by their obedience to Him. It is unsurprising that the command in Leviticus 18:5 is reproduced throughout the sacred Scriptures, and reflected in the New Testament, especially in the writings of the Apostle John. God spoke through the prophet Ezekiel regarding apostate Israel: "And I gave them my statutes, and shewed them my judgments, which if a man do, he shall even live in them" (Ezekiel 20:11). Obedience to God's law for the children of Israel was presented as a non-negotiable necessity for those who would please God.

The Word of God calls us to a reverential and practical love of God's commandments in this age of spiritual declension and widespread lawlessness. Ignoring or minimising God's law remains a harbinger of death (Matt. 5:19), for Romans describes the law as "holy, and just, and good" (7:12) and even "spiritual" (7:14). As one has said, "God's law is like a manufacturer's manual showing human beings how to act according to their nature... breaking God's law is just like running into the wall or jumping from the plane without a parachute."[55]   Rather, the new nature finds it no burden to "run in the way of thy commandments" (Ps. 119:32).

Can Hedonism Engender Holiness?

The command to obey God's law appears many times in the New Testament in many forms, being either assumed or directly expressed; in New Calvinism, however, a preoccupation with obedience often seems *anathema*. The repetitive use of the theme "the gospel" in New Calvinism often belies a distaste for what is portrayed as the opposite to "the gospel": the law. Similarly, a meticulous approach to keeping the law is widely portrayed as being out of character and indeed the pole opposite to what is truly desirable and the epitome of holiness: preoccupation with "the gospel."

The New Calvinist "gospel-centred" approach is especially

clear in the writings of Timothy Keller, one of the most prominent apologists in the New Calvinist movement. A Presbyterian minister in New York, Keller rose to popular fame in 2008 for his book *The Reason for God* on the subject of apologetics, adopting an ecumenical approach in his answering the critics of religion. Keller's theology of salvation is especially clear in his book *The Prodigal God*, also published in 2008, where he presents the "obedient" elder brother as being a worse sinner than the prodigal son, and makes this the novel basis on which the whole parable should be interpreted. Keller calls this the "heart of the Christian faith which must be recovered."[56]

Similar to Keller, a new approach to duty undergirds the whole theology of John Piper with his emphasis on the presence of personal pleasure (hedonism) as central to experiencing a right relationship with God.

At the heart of hedonism is a heresy: this doctrine does not engender the holiness of which the Scriptures speak and "without which no man shall see the Lord" (Heb. 12:14). John Piper's most devoted fans and followers are likely to be rocking out to pagan superstars. In January 2017, John Piper preached to 55,000 young people on the same stage as same-sex marriage advocate and American Idol sensation Carrie Underwood. Back in 2012, MTV

> In January 2017, Piper shared a stage at Passion 2017 with American Idol sensation and same-sex marriage advocate Carrie Underwood.

dubbed Underwood as "the latest public figure to come out in support of gay marriage."[57] She stated: "I definitely think we should all have the right to love, and love publicly, the people that we want to love." The pagan Underwood claimed her support for same-sex marriage was "actually a result of her Christian values, not in conflict with them."

Thus, John Piper has reduced the Christian youth to fools: they are entranced by his hedonist rambling while being entertained by an advocate for the greatest assault on Scripture of our day. The Lord Jesus declared of Sodom and Gomorrah, the cities renowned for same-sex activity, that God "rained fire and brimstone from heaven and destroyed them all" (Luke 17:29). Piper brings young people together, however, to be entertained by an artist who promotes opposition to Christ's commands. Underwood is an opponent of God, but Piper, though sharing the stage with her, would have us believe that he is God's messenger.

Piper is often hailed as one of the greatest "preachers" of his generation, and in 2010 was described in a festschrift as "one of the extraordinary pastors of our generation."[58] John MacArthur, for example, has said that he, since 1988, has "read and followed [John Piper's] ministry with joy and gratitude."[59]

Piper's legacy for January 2017, however, was to appear on stage at the Passion Conference for ministry with a same-sex marriage advocate, Carrie Underwood. Does anyone care as to the effect that this has on the minds of the estimated 50,000 young people who assembled in Atlanta, Georgia at Passion 2017? Would any analyst of his theology feel that perhaps Piper's ministry would be best evaluated by his choice of stage companion?

In Scripture, the law and the gospel are contrasted only as ways by which man seeks salvation. Considered in their proper context, however, the law and the gospel complement one another, and are both valuable and useful to the Christian in his or her desire to please God. Paul was the Apostle inspired of the Holy Ghost to articulate the doctrine of justification by faith. Yet, it was him who declared that he exercised himself to "have always a conscience void of offence toward God, and toward men" (Acts 24:16). The measure to which his life conformed to God's just demands weighed heavily upon Paul. Not only so, he publicly testified to his accomplishment in living a holy life, both before unbelievers (Acts 23:1) and the church (Acts 20:26).

Arthur Pink declared that "the law of God expresses the mind of the Creator... and is God's unchanging moral standard for regulating the conduct of all men."[60] The moral law was not given to save man, but to show him his sin (Rom. 3:23) and need of salvation (Gal. 3:19). An attack on God's law is an attack on God Himself. Against every attack, however, the law of God endures as a radiant display of the need of man (1 Tim. 1:9), the glory of the cross (Jn. 1:17), and the reality of coming judgment (Rev. 20:12).

> The measure to which his life conformed to God's just demands weighed heavily upon Paul.

The doctrine of John Piper is a departure from the old truths and simple message which the church has always declared: "as many as received Him, to them gave He power to become the sons of God" (Jn. 1:12). The gospel preached in its true glory engenders an evangelical obedience which delights to follow God's commands. Repentance that leads to salvation (2 Cor. 7:10) is no sentimental feeling, neither is it a fruitless intellectual endeavour. Rather, it is the holy work of God the Spirit in the heart. John Piper's doctrine, considered as a whole, and not in isolated statements, is bereft of the authority of the Word of God on sin, the futility of the flesh (be it in Mother Teresa or the hedonistic pagan), the law of God, and the absolute necessity of holiness. It is little wonder, as Passion 2017 demonstrated, that it leaves its adherents in a worse state than it found them (Luke 11: 26).

Those that have broken the fences of modesty will never be held by the bonds of piety.

MATTHEW HENRY

4 | The Fruits of John Piper

*Trees whose fruit withereth, without fruit, twice
dead, plucked up by the roots.*
JUDE 12

Matthew Henry, the nonconformist Bible commentator of
the 17th century, wrote regarding sexual sin:

Can anything be more inconsistent with our profession or
relation? ...The sin of fornication is a great injury in a Christian
to his Head and Lord, and a great reproach and blot on his
profession. It is no wonder therefore that the apostle should
say, "Flee fornication (1 Cor. 6:18), avoid it, keep out of the
reach of temptations to it, of provoking objects. Direct the eyes
and mind to other things and thoughts." *Alia vitia pugnando,*

sola libido fugiendo vincitur — Other vices may be conquered in fight, this only by flight; so speak many of the fathers.[61]

When I served as leader of the Christian Union on the campus of NUI Galway, we held many public talks throughout the year on subjects ranging from the reliability of the Scriptures to the problem of pain in a world which God created. Towards the end of the academic year, the Students' Union on campus put a motion to the entire student body. This motion, if successful, would mandate the union to push for "same-sex" marriage nationwide. As students, and members of the Students' Union, this was something we could not countenance. We covenanted, as the Christians on campus, to mount a simple counter-campaign.

Never have I seen such opposition to Christianity as I saw following the launch of our campaign. Our table on the main concourse of the college was vandalised within hours, and practically all our posters ripped down. Members of the Christian Union were physically intimidated and the object of vitriolic abuse and threats in person and on social media (one user said I should be doused in petrol and set alight). The fury of hell was vented against our message that marriage was a lifelong union between one man and one woman. We had touched a raw nerve and the devil's wrath was unleashed. Even a year later, students who had observed us on the day continued to comment publicly on how badly we had been treated.

Men of God throughout the ages have acknowledged that any true work of God will bring opposition. Paul, however, makes that great statement of the twofold Christian influence: "to the one we are the savour of death unto death; and to the other the savour of life unto life" (2 Cor. 2:16). In 1791, John Wesley warned Wilberforce that unless God endued him with power for the battle against slavery, he would be "worn out by the opposition of men and devils."[62]

Fruit: The Practical Effect of Teaching

Christ commands in Matthew 7:15 to "beware of false prophets" but follows up with an instruction as to how we are to keep His command: "ye shall know them by their fruits" (Mt. 7:16). Testing the prophets (or teachers) of our day is not a complicated task beyond the reach of the Christian, but a command which Christ expects and empowers us to fulfil.

> In 1791, John Wesley warned Wilberforce that unless God endued him with power for the battle against slavery, he would be "worn out by the opposition of men and devils."

The word fruit in the New Testament, karpos, means fruit, produce or crop. It is used widely all throughout the New Testament, especially in the gospels. The Brown, Fausset and Jamieson Commentary notes that by fruits is meant "not their doctrines—as many of the elder interpreters and some later ones explain it—for that corresponds to the tree itself; but the practical effect of their teaching, which is the proper fruit of the tree."[63]

Measuring, or assessing, the "practical effect" of the teaching of John Piper and other New Calvinists is thus commanded

63

by the Lord Jesus Christ and the duty of every Christian.

There is no doubt that the teaching of John Piper and other New Calvinists is bearing fruit, i.e. is having a practical effect on the church. That is not to say that it is having a favourable effect, for the evidence shows an extremely negative impact, when measured against the rule of God's Word. Nonetheless, even the secular media has recognised that New Calvinism is having an impact: a landmark article published in Time magazine included "The New Calvinism" in its "Ten Ideas Changing the World Right Now" and mentioning a trio of leaders: "the pioneering new-Calvinist John Piper of Minneapolis, Seattle's pugnacious Mark Driscoll and Albert Mohler, head of the Southern Seminary of the huge Southern Baptist Convention."[64]

> "The practical effect of teaching is the proper fruit of the tree."

Perhaps one of the clearest practical effects of John Piper's teaching is the new attitude towards the discussion, and sometimes doing, of practices which were once considered taboo in Christian circles. One example is tattoos: Piper holds that the injunction on "printing any marks" on the body in Leviticus 19:28 is not binding on the Christian today[65] (his son, Barnabas Piper, has a tattoo and gives advice on choosing one). Mark Driscoll, a close friend of John Piper's, promoted tattoos for years while leading Mars Hill Church in Seattle, blasphemously declaring that the Lord Jesus Christ would be wearing a tattoo on His second coming to earth.[66] Another, more significant example of change fostered by New

Calvinism is found in Piper's attitude towards sexual sin: Piper and his contemporary New Calvinists discuss the subject in-depth, with almost no topic off-limits, conversing ad lib on a whole array of sexual subjects which the Scripture says ought not be mentioned.

The New Laxity Towards Sexual Sin

Many of the sternest commands in Scripture surround illicit sexual relationships. Paul commanded to "flee fornication" (1 Cor. 6:18), distinguishing it from other sins as especially destructive. The writer of Hebrews warned that God would surely judge "whoremongers (the sexually immoral) and adulterers" (Heb. 13:4). In the Old Testament, the exemplary Joseph escaped the temptress' advances, exclaiming "How then can I do this great wickedness, and sin against God?" (Gen. 39:9). Joseph tolerated no mental debate. He facilitated no dialogue. He simply fled. Moses is remembered for "choosing rather to suffer affliction with the people of God, than to enjoy the pleasures of sin for a season" (Heb. 11:25).

Today, however, in most churches, this attitude no longer prevails. Despite the exhortation of the Apostle Paul to Timothy to "keep thyself pure" (1 Tim. 5:22), there is surprisingly little difference between the lifestyle of the professing Christian and that of the world at large. The music, entertainment, and fashions of the world are normal for churchgoing young people, as is the accompanying sexual sin that goes along with them.

Can a concrete link be drawn between the proliferation of Piper's teaching and the laxity towards sexual sin now tolerated in the church? I believe that it can. One of the firmest indications of such a link, I believe, lies in the unscriptural and irresponsible discussion of sin which is promoted (not just tolerated) in New Calvinism. When the church begins to discuss what was once earmarked as unspeakable sin, the church has changed its attitude towards that sin, and practical effects will surely follow.

Piper's Approach Towards the Discussion of Sex

History shows that beginning to discuss the unthinkable is the first step to eventually having it normalised, legalised and popularised in society. Katherine Zappone, the American-born Irish Minister for Children and Youth Affairs, is an avowed secularist whose mission is to abolish any interference between church and state in Ireland. She was instrumental in the campaign leading to the legalisation of same-sex marriage in Ireland (May 2015). During a recent interview, Zappone signalled that the discussion of same-sex relations by the media was the first step in changing public opinion, as it "started the conversation."[67]

> The discussion of same-sex relations was the first step in chaning public opinion.

Just like Zappone and other proponents of change, Piper has initiated conversation about sex into the language of the church, talking about it like the world does, and breaking down the walls surrounding the sanctity of sex. His website, Desiring God, contains hundreds of articles on subjects which Christians should, according to Scripture, not "make mention of." Piper conducts his discussion under the guise of attempting to help those in sin, but nonetheless, he has succeeded in normalising discussion of such topics among Christians when this was once not the case. This new approach towards discussion of sex, in particular, is a prominent feature of almost all New Calvinist authors. John Piper has made the church (especially the younger generation) more comfortable in openly conversing on sexual matters.

The devil knows that all that is needed is for the church to capitulate to the point of discussing what God has forbidden. One compromise will then lead to another. The tragedy of 21st century Western culture is the proliferation of sexual degradation in all its forms. New Calvinists have today popularised open discussion of markedly intimate matters in the pulpit and the sanctuary. As early as the 1980s, Piper began writing openly about sexual sins in a casual manner and this has been a feature of his writing since that time.[68]

The Scripture records that Balaam, having failed to curse God's people, drew them into sexual sin with the women of Midian and so accomplished his initial aim in a subtler way. Balaam was wiser, in a sense, than the Israelites: he knew that their unique purity lay at the heart of their relationship to God and was their greatest defence (Num. 23:8-10). Israel yielded to the overtures of the strange women, were overcome, and perished in their sin.

Modesty and restraint, in language and in life, is a great defence of the Christian against the world, the flesh, and the devil. Matthew Henry once famously commented: "Those that have broken the fences of modesty will never be held by the bonds of piety."[69]

How deep his insight was! Having lost their inhibition of close alliance and sexual contact with the women of Midian, they were soon bowing down to their idols, and committing the ultimate rejection of Jehovah (Num. 25:1,2). So, comments Henry, "those that have dishonoured themselves by fleshly lusts will not scruple to dishonour God by idolatrous worships."

How interesting that, in like fashion to Balaam (Jude 11), John Piper has combined extolling of the doctrines of the Reformed faith with revelling to the beat of musicians espousing a wholly pagan view of sexual relationships.[70] Thus, holy doctrine has been firmly wedded to unholy practise to form a toxic concoction born in hell. This is a work of the devil and not of God. Sensuality is poisonous fruit with an evil root. As the 19th century expositor James Ramsey declared, "Sensuality and idolatry in some form or other are the invariable results of error. Whether apostasy begins in a secret covetousness or in doctrinal error it ends up in the same horrid depths of moral pollution."[71]

> Holy doctrine has been firmly wedded to unholy practice.

Piper's Unscriptural View that
Guilt, Not Sin, is the Problem

When one examines the core of Piper's message on sexual sin, it becomes clear that a different message from that of preachers in generations gone by is being articulated. Piper assumes that young Christians will be sinning sexually and tailors his message to that end. A close examination of his writing reveals that, to Piper, the main tragedy of sexual sin is not the offense which it causes to God but the guilt which it leaves in the conscience. Piper explicitly states such heresy over and over in his sermons and articles.

An example of this is found in an article which Piper penned in 2007. Writing in *Christianity Today*, he titled his article: "Gutsy Guilt: Don't let shame over sexual sin destroy you." In his article, Piper declares: 'The great tragedy is not ... fornication or pornography. The tragedy is that Satan uses guilt from these failures to strip you of every radical dream you ever had or might have."[72]

Here, Piper seems far more concerned to combat the *effects* of sexual sin than to condemn the heinousness of the sin itself. Ultimately, he teaches a psychological soothing of the guilt of sin while downplaying its seriousness.

Piper's use of emotive language, with an emphasis on liberation ("seeing Jesus") and "Christian" hedonism, counters Scripture's clear pronouncements on the gross error and tragedy of sexual sin. His message is attractive to young people, many of whom have no genuine experience of salvation, or are backslidden and are attracted by the pleasures of the world. The practical effect of Piper's preaching is to leave Christians, especially Christian young people, with less fear of sexual sin, and less inhibition in persisting along its path. This is a snare to the church, not a blessing, a ploy which will sap its youth of strength, and a cancer which will eat out the vitals of Christian testimony.

Piper's statements on sexual sin are wholly unscriptural. In 1984, he stated regarding sexual sin that "Periodic failure in this area no more disqualifies you from ministry than periodic failures of impatience."[73]

Proverbs, however, repeatedly associates sexual sin with spiritual death. Proverbs 7 warns regarding the harlot that "she hath cast down many wounded: yea, many strong men have been slain by her; her house is the way to hell, going down to the chambers of death" (7:26-27). The guests of the harlot are portrayed as being in the depths of hell (Pro. 9:18) and there is a certain doom repeatedly attached to their destiny: "He that doeth it destroyeth his own soul; a wound and dishonour shall he get; and his reproach shall not be wiped away" (6:32-33).

A faithful holding forth of the word of God will testify to the full seriousness of sin as revealed in Scripture. Sexual sin, according to the book of Proverbs, leaves stains impossible to remove: "His own iniquities shall take the wicked himself, and he shall be holden with the cords of his sins; he shall die without instruction; and in the greatness of his folly he shall go astray" (5:22-23). While there is hope for any repentant sinner, the emphasis in Scripture is always on judgment when it comes to sexual sin.

This new approach to sexual sin is a philosophy that runs like a thread through all of Piper's teaching, and is not an isolated doctrine. Speaking at the Passion Conference in Atlanta in 2007, John Piper again reiterated his philosophy. He stated regarding young people: "the great tragedy is not mainly...fornication...the tragedy is that Satan uses the guilt of these failures to strip you of every radical dream you ever had."[74] Piper accomplishes a subtle shift in emphasis here, moving his condemnation away from the sin itself to the effects of the sin. Piper states explicitly in the same speech: "my aim is not mainly to cure you of sexual misconduct... you need to fall on your face and plead that God would open your eyes to see the compelling glory of Jesus Christ."

Piper's words reveal a move away from the scriptural view of sin, however. Curing sexual misconduct *ought to be* the aim of every preacher, for curing the sinner of his sin was the reason for Christ's coming (Mt. 1:21), and sin is the "transgression of the law" (1 Jn. 3:4). The power of Christ's gospel *is seen* in the sinner being cured of sexual misconduct, and all other transgressions of God's law.

The Consequences of Taking Sin Lightly

Any departure from the clear doctrines of Scripture amounts to spiritual poison, and poison has harmful consequences. Piper's words have the effect of downplaying the slavery inherent in sexual sin, and the curse on those who persist in it. Furthermore, in downplaying these realities, he downplays the fear of sin in those who listen to him, and thus does them spiritual harm. In this regard, he is guilty of the same sin as those teachers mentioned by the Apostle Peter: "they allure through the lusts of the flesh, through much wantonness, those that were clean escaped from them who live in error; while they promise them liberty, they themselves are the servants of corruption: for of whom a man is overcome, of the same is he brought in bondage" (2 Peter 2:18-19).

> The power of Christ's gospel is seen in the sinner being cured of sexual misconduct, and all other transgressions of God's law.

With Piper, one hears little of the vengeance of God against those who indulge in the sin of the age (Rev. 21:8), or the attitude which God commands that the church adopt towards such sin in its midst: "put away from among yourselves that wicked person" (1 Cor. 5:13). Sexual sin is singled out in Scripture for particularly vigilant avoidance: "Flee fornication. Every sin that a man doeth is without the body; but he that committeth fornication sinneth against his own body" (1 Cor. 6:18). This is the sentiment that any faithful preacher will urge upon his congregation. The first step of entanglement in such sin has fearful consequences: the church therefore should flee the voice of strangers such as John Piper (Jn. 10:5) and remember that if one becomes ensnared, "the last state of that man is worse than the first" (Mt. 12:45).

The Corrupting Influence of a False Teacher

Piper's doctrine of taking sexual sin lightly is evident from the lives of his followers and allies; nowhere is this clearer, perhaps, than in his friend and fellow-teacher Mark Driscoll, originally from Seattle, Washington, now pastor of The Trinity Church in Scottsdale, Arizona. While in Seattle, Mark Driscoll established such a reputation for profanity and free discussion of sexual immorality that even many secular commentators found his taste obsessive and crude. In 2012, Driscoll appeared on CNN to talk to host Piers Morgan about his new book on marriage: Morgan commented "there's a lot of sex in this book...unusually for a man of cloth, you're keen on it."[75] Driscoll's book on marriage, includes graphic descriptions and deep discussions of things which should not be mentioned.[76] Eventually, Driscoll's perversion and depravity caused his own congregation to move against him in August 2014.

Piper's close relationship with Mark Driscoll indicates what Piper's teaching looks like in practice, when the emotive language of Christian Hedonism is stripped away. Despite the fact that Driscoll's levity, irreverence and immorality has polluted the minds of thousands of young people (many of Driscoll's videos have over 100,000 views on social media), Piper has not distanced himself from him, but rather aligned himself to him all the more. Asked in November 2014 about Driscoll, Piper made his position clear: "No regret. John Piper has no regret for befriending Mark Driscoll, going to Mark Driscoll's church and speaking at his events, or having him come to the Desiring God conference."[77]

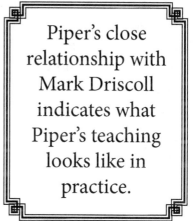

Piper's close relationship with Mark Driscoll indicates what Piper's teaching looks like in practice.

Piper has arguably presided over the greatest demise in the holiness of the church, especially amongst its youth, since the Reformation. Like the serpent, Piper has subtly presented Christian youth as blind to a better good: "your eyes shall be opened" (Gen. 3:5). He predicates this, like the serpent, on denying the commandments of God, and on downplaying the fear of God. To Piper, God's commandments and the keeping thereof is not a beautiful thing (1 John 5:3). It is not the essence of God's love. Rather, keeping God's commandments is an obstacle to having our eyes opened to "something greater" – a hedonistic approach to God.

The devil was playing on words when he spoke to Eve. Eve was not able for him and neither are most Christians able for Piper. His sermons contain truth, as the devil's words did, but not God's full truth. "Ye shall not surely die" (Genesis 3:4), the devil said, and indeed Eve did not die physically the moment she tasted the fruit. However, what God had said came to pass. On eating the fruit, Adam and Eve became spiritually dead, just as God had warned, and their physical bodies also began a downward spiral. This foretold death would eventually pass to all men (Rom. 5:12).

The serpent used an appeal to pseudo-logic and this also is Piper's most dazzling weapon. The devil said "surely", i.e. that doesn't make sense. He held out the gold nugget of deeper knowledge "ye shall be as gods, knowing good and evil." Piper's sermons are laced with philosophy and psychology but weak on historical theology and Christian doctrine, and most of all, weak on Scriptural exegesis. This is no surprise: Piper's first degree minored in philosophy at Wheaton College where he studied under men such as Clyde Kilby, one of the world's most prominent scholars of C.S. Lewis. Lewis appealed to a generation of churchgoers who had forsaken God's commandments and were looking for a religion acceptable to the world. Fifty years later, Piper has done the same for an apostate Christendom that is desperate to please the world and live in harmony with it.

The Devil's Strategy to Cripple the Church

The end of sin is always *death*. The result of every false teacher is a crippled church. It was said of Adam and Eve that "the eyes of them both were opened, and they knew that they were naked"

(Gen. 3:7). We can dress up sin under the guise of "liberty" but sin ensnares, and a sinning church is a dying church in subjection to the world, and enslaved to sin. Slaves cannot lead, rebuke, or challenge. They hide in the background (Gen. 3:8).

The church ought to be characterised by its life (Jn. 10:10) and its crystal-clear proclamation of God's truth to a fallen world. Neither Piper nor his followers emulate such life; rather, the opposite is the case. In 2012, as previously noted, Piper even refused to take a position on a referendum to define marriage as a union between one man and one woman in his home state of Minnesota.[78] This, surely, is not the faith of God's elect, but the fruit of a poisoned chalice. A weakened view of sin makes one weak on missions, weak on evangelism, and weak on proclaiming God's truth in the public square, because sin slowly but surely enslaves its victims. Worldliness in the church ushers in *rigor mortis* and renders it powerless to rebuke the world.

As the fictitious Pied Piper lured the unsuspecting children of Hamelin to promised good fortune, so also John Piper lures many to a lighter view of sin, a lighter view of holiness, and a lighter view of the reality of God's wrath. The gloss of Piper's doctrine contains appeal for those who are not firmly acquainted with the truth, and who have not been mastered by it. The charm of Piper's message captivates

> John Piper lures many to a lighter view of sin, a lighter view of holiness, and a lighter view of the reality of God's wrath.

75

those who would escape the cost of discipleship and hear new, wrested interpretations of the things of God which are "hard to be understood" (2 Pet. 3:16).

The Pied Piper of Hamelin, however, lured his victims to their doom. Charmed by the music of the Piper's flute, the children were lured from the safety of Hamelin, oblivious to the foolishness of their actions, and so perished. So also, those who follow Piper are taking a well-worn path to destruction, for to take God's word lightly is to invite His judgment. An embrace of Piper's doctrine is an embrace of "doctrines of devils" and a courting of eternal destruction. Young Christians should turn from the tune of this false prophet, and heed instead the exhortation of Scripture to "exercise thyself rather unto godliness" (1 Tim. 4:7) and to be an "example of the believers, in word, in conversation, in charity, in spirit, in faith, in purity" (1 Tim. 4:12).

You can never get a man out of a bog-hole
by going in beside him.
W. P. Nicholson

5 | Taking Back the Church

Judgment must begin at the house of God.

I Peter 4:17

It is time to take back the church from the hirelings and the heretics. A Christianity without a "contending for the faith" is not genuine Christianity at all (Jude 3). In all great times of revival in the church, there has been a common theme of "judgment beginning at the house of God" (1 Pet. 4:17).

In the early 16th century, Luther opened his mouth to declare God's truth against the might of the Roman Catholic monstrosity.

79

He stood in contrast to those who had highlighted Rome's abuses but failed to condemn them outright. Ronald Bainton, the acclaimed biographer of German reformer Martin Luther, declared regarding Luther's writing of the 95 Theses in October 1517: "Luther's Theses differed from the ordinary propositions for debate...The ninety-five affirmations are crisp, bold, unqualified."[79]

Luther rose up to speak the truth in his day, publicly proclaiming his 95 Theses and God blessed his stand with a glorious Reformation. When the people of God take upon themselves their individual responsibility for the truth, God hears from heaven and rewards mightily (Heb. 11:6).

The change in the church's attitude towards truth in the last half-century has caused it to forfeit the blessing of God. Compromise and accommodation are now the order of the day. These traits, however, are fatal to the church. The renowned Ulster evangelist of the early 20th century, William P. Nicholson, once railed against what he described as the "Peril of a Compromising Policy" in a sermon which he preached entitled "The Christian's Perils". He declared:

> You get an invitation to a card party... You have no love for the thing, but it is a delicate situation, and you say, "Well, I will go. I will not dance, I will just sit and look on... I want to show friendliness and I will go. I would like to help these friends of mine to Christ." But you can never get a man out of a bog-hole by going in beside him.[80]

Nicholson went on to contrast the characters of Abraham and

Lot, depicting the younger as arguing "You will never do any good up here; the common-sense thing is to go down and make yourself one of them", and the Patriarch as saying "No...I will stay by my sheep." The preacher recounts how that, though Lot went down to Sodom to do "some social service work", the tragic end of the matter was the rise of the Moabites and Ammonites who were "thorns in the sides of Israel ever afterwards."[81] Nicholson witnessed the peril of compromise in his day destroying many Christian lives, and the problem has surely grown fourfold since the days in which he ministered.

Serving a Holy God in an Immoral World

The God that we serve is a thrice-holy God. Scripture makes clear that holiness becometh the saints of God in all aspects of their lives, but especially the sexual realm: "For this is the will of God, even your sanctification, that ye should abstain from fornication; that every one of you should know how to possess his vessel in sanctification and honour; not in the lust of concupiscence, even as the Gentiles which know not God" (1 Thess. 4:3-5).

God demands that His people be pure in their relationships, and reject the sexual norms of the world in which they live (Lev. 18: 26-30). Orthodoxy of doctrine unaccompanied by holiness of life is no guard against the God who promises to judge all whoremongers and adulterers (Heb. 13:4).

To indulge in sexual sins is to live and act as those outside of Christ and with no knowledge of the one true God, whose will is our sanctification and abstinence from fornication. "Keep thyself pure" was Paul's exhortation to the young Timothy, while John declared that the Christian who longs for Christ's coming "purifieth himself, even as He is pure" (I John 3:3). Impurity, by contrast, is inextricably linked with damnation: the Bible warns that "no whoremonger, nor unclean person...hath any inheritance in the kingdom of Christ and of God" (Eph. 5:3-5).

We witness today the rise of organised, vociferous opposition to the sexual mores of the Scripture. Young people are actively encouraged to explicitly discuss sexual beliefs and to rebel against the Christian morals they have been taught. The secular agenda of those who have excluded God from their imagination (Rom. 1:21, 28) is to create a world devoid of moral restraint, where people are free to indulge their sexual lusts. The Bible, to the contrary, condemns sexual sin in all its impurity, and warns that human sexual behaviour is subject to the law of God. Fornication, adultery, and homosexuality are all topics about which parents should instruct their children in the right ways of the Lord, counselling them to conduct themselves in a way which honours Him.

> We witness today the rise of organised, vociferous opposition to the sexual mores of the Scripture.

Reviving Church Discipline

Christ warned the church in Thyatira regarding its toleration of Jezebel in Revelation 2:20. Such toleration provided cover for Jezebel, "which calleth herself a prophetess, to teach and to seduce my servants to commit fornication." Thus, as early as the first century, sinister teachers were at work in the church seeking to undermine the purity of its people. These had adopted an air of authority (Jezebel the *prophetess*) and duped the early church.

The Scripture gives clear instructions on how the church ought to discipline those within its fold who persist in sexual sin. The Apostle Paul declares in 1 Corinthians 5:

> I have written unto you not to keep company, if any man that is called a brother be a fornicator…with such an one no not to eat. For what have I to do to judge them also that are without? do not ye judge them that are within? But them that are without God judgeth. Therefore put away from among yourselves that wicked person. (v. 11-13)

Paul mandated that there be a complete break of fellowship by the church with those who were called "brethren" but who chose to continue in sin: "put away from among yourselves that wicked person" (v13). "Cast him out of your fellowship," one commentator said, "and avoid his conversation."[82] The church is to *judge* the fornicator in its midst. Today it is more common to make them feel welcome, overlook their open sin, and avoid asking them the hard questions a true pastor should. Hence, we fly in the face of God's word and take the curse of God unto ourselves.

Many today argue that false professors will always be in the church and that the presence of such amongst believers is no cause for great concern: this sentiment is in flagrant opposition to that of the Apostle Paul, however. Paul's concern here was not with doctrinal heresy in the Corinthian Church, but with the practical failure of the church to discipline a man in open sin in their midst (1 Cor. 5:1-2). This failure Paul condemned outright. Paul did not urge the believers to simply keep themselves individually from the corrupting influence of this man. He did not say that there would always be a sinner or two in their congregation, but that as long as they kept their statement of faith doctrinally pure they were walking in obedience to God. No! Rather, he exhorted them to, when assembled together, collectively remove this source of corruption from their midst (1 Cor. 5:3-5).

> Paul's primary concern in 1 Corinthians 5 was not with doctrinal heresy, but with the practical failure to discipline a man in open sin in their midst.

God's word will rise up on the last day and be our judge if we refuse to hold the church to the same standard in our generation. The Apostle Paul did not mention doctrine in this passage; the doctrinal position of the Corinthian Church was not his primary concern here. Rather, he mentioned "deed" (1 Cor. 5:2-3). Twice the flagrant sin of this man in their midst, the knowledge of which was in the public domain, was called to the attention of the Corinthian believers. Paul demanded that they conclusively deal with this open sin and gave clear instructions on how to deal with the fornicator. He did not propose formulating a church assembly to consider a new doctrinal statement, or an addition to the church's statement of faith, but rather commanded that the fornicator be excommunicated from the church (1 Cor. 5:5, 13).

Sexual sin is the sin of our age; yet, how little we hear, if ever, of such procedures being followed in the church today. Discipline of this hue is non-existent in most churches: the church therefore has become corrupted and cursed of God. Matthew Henry felt the burden of the church's responsibility in this regard; he declared, "the sins of such [wicked professors] much more dishonour God than the sins of the openly wicked and profane can do. The church therefore is obliged to clear herself from all confederacy with them, or connivance at them, and to bear testimony against their wicked practices."[83]

God calls the church, and especially its ministers and leaders, to take decisive action against sin and scandal in its midst. Faithful church discipline has always been a defining characteristic of a legitimate church. Ramsey declared regarding the same: "The worship of a true and living church or believer, and the faithful discipline of such a church...these two go together. They never can be separated...[and] are essential and characteristic elements of every true church. The possession of these make her a church; the want of these is proof of apostasy."[84] How fearful then if the church be found wanting in this most holy task! The unmistakeable clarity of God's instruction on this subject is all the more reason for the church to forsake its sin, repudiate its lop-sidedness, and recover this vital element of its being.

The Capitulation of the Church

During the latter half of the twentieth century, true biblical Christianity was known for the care in which it held the church. The rise of modernism and ecumenism strengthened the church's conviction that the truth was under attack, and rallied its determination to protect against infiltration at all costs. Dr Brian Green, a late President of the separatist British Council of Protestant Christian Churches, exemplified this duty of care when he warned his generation of the need to be ever "aware of the insidious infiltration of the Roman Church into Protestantism."[85]

From the mid-1960s onwards, strongholds of biblical truth all around the world capitulated to ecumenism and neo-evangelicalism. This was especially clear in North America, as church after church and seminary after seminary lost clarity on cardinal doctrines such as biblical inerrancy, personal holiness of life, biblical separation from error, and substitutionary atonement.

Northern Ireland's Free Presbyterian Church

One exception to this general trend was Northern Ireland, where a consolidation of support for the fundamentals of the faith emerged in Protestantism amid political conflict. In the early 1950s, the firebrand preacher Ian Paisley emerged as the de facto leader of the faithful in Northern Ireland. Rev. Paisley would later famously describe Northern Ireland as the "the last bastion of Protestantism in Europe."[86] Rev. Paisley's ministry in Northern Ireland in the 60s, 70s and 80s

> The Free Presbyterian church was at the centre of the battle against compromise for most of the late twentieth century.

encouraged Christians to take a bold stand for the fundamentals of the faith and resist heresy, apostasy and spiritual compromise. Many were won to Christ, and missions, revival meetings and Bible conferences were commonplace across the province of Ulster.

The Free Presbyterian Church, which Ian Paisley founded in 1951, was at the centre of the battle against compromise for most of the late twentieth century. It preached vociferously against the evils, not just of Romanism, but also of an apostate Protestantism that compromised with error. The congregations of the early Free Presbyterian churches were often those who had left other professedly evangelical churches which had capitulated to modernism, worldliness of life, or ecumenism. As a result, Free Presbyterians were widely vilified by many professing Christians and by the wider world, scorned both for their uncompromising stand against the evils of the day and their rousing call to holiness of life.

There are signs to suggest, however, that the Free Presbyterian Church is no longer characterised by such militancy for the truth. The Free Presbyterian website, recently redesigned and modernised, contains the same doctrinal statements as ever. In practice, however, it is no longer known for its uncompromising stand against spiritual declension. Gardenstown Free Presbyterian Church in Scotland, for example, reproduces on its website a whole blog post by J. I. Packer, an Anglican evangelical who is well known for his participation in the ecumenical movement. In 1995, Packer contributed to a book entitled Evangelicals and Catholics Together: Towards a Common Mission. Packer signed the ECT declaration in 1994 and the later Manhattan Declaration in 2009, both documents produced by close cooperation between Roman Catholics and evangelicals.

Once the Free Presbyterian witness was synonymous with a vigorous repudiation of all ecumenism and ecclesiastical compromise. However, many Free Presbyterian churches now host speakers in their churches who are not separatist, the most prominent example being Joel Beeke of Grand Rapids, Michigan. Beeke was invited by John Piper to address the Desiring God National Conference in 2011, where Piper promoted Beeke's books enthusiastically from the lectern. John Piper gave Beeke a glowing introduction before he came to speak, stating "I am deeply thankful that Dr Joel Beeke has been willing to come and minister" and Dr Beeke later thanked Piper and referred to him as a "brother."[87]

> Joel Beeke has participated widely in a variety of ecumenical initiatives and has also spoken in the Free Presbyterian Church on a number of occasions.

Beeke has also participated widely in a variety of ecumenical initiatives, most notably Refo500. Refo500, organised by Dutch scholar Herman Selderhuis, is an international effort to commemorate the 500th anniversary of the Reformation. [88] The openly ecumenical nature of the effort is seen in the variety of Roman Catholic and Protestant partners listed, including the Institute for Ecumenical Research, the Jesuit Historical Society in Africa, and Fuller Theological Seminary. Refo500 was launched in 2010 in Gouda, in the Netherlands, and featured a Roman Catholic

Jesuit priest, Dr. Antoine Bodar, as one of the opening speakers. Bodar, whose lecture is available online, titled his address "Back to the One Church" and declared that the Reformation was "because of reform, progress; due to schism, mistake."[89]

Beeke is still associated with Refo500; at the time of writing, the latest blog post on the English Refo500 website is an advertisement of Beeke's "Rhine River Reformation Cruise" in July 2018 (prices start at $5,899 from Chicago). The cruise will involve theological addresses by Beeke and two other speakers. Beeke was a featured speaker at a Refo500 conference in August 2016 at the Theological University of Apeldoorn in the Netherlands.[90] As for Herman Selderhuis, Beeke has closely collaborated with this man, the Director of Refo500, for years. Beeke wrote a glowing endorsement of Selderhuis' biography of Martin Luther (2017), has contributed to a primer on Reformed Orthodoxy edited by Selderhuis (2013), and just recently announced a "strategic partnership" between the seminary which he is President of (Puritan Reformed Theological Seminary) and the university which Selderhuis is Rector of, the Theological University of Apeldoorn.[91]

> Free Presbyterian minister John Greer collaborated closely with Joel Beeke in the production of the Reformation Heritage Study Bible, and has had Beeke as a guest speaker in his Ballymena church.

Notwithstanding Beeke's ecumenical ties, Free Presbyterian ministers have worked closely with him. John Greer is the minister of Ballymena Free Presbyterian Church, one of the largest Free Presbyterian congregations in Northern Ireland. Greer collaborated with Beeke on the production of the Reformation Heritage Study Bible published in 2014.[92] Beeke has also spoken at Greer's church in Ballymena, as well as at Mount Merrion Free Presbyterian Church in Belfast. It is sad to see such close communion between Free Presbyterians and Beeke, a man now well-known for his ecumenical connections, especially as the Free Presbyterian Church was once renowned for its faithful and uncompromising stand.

Is Eulogising Martin Luther Sincere?

In August 2017, a young Christian student attending Oxford University became aware of the fact that Free Presbyterian ministers were scheduled to share a platform at a UK Bible conference with an Oxford Baptist pastor, Derrick Morlan, who had preached at Roman Catholic funerals. This student contacted the leadership of the Free Presbyterian Church in Northern Ireland, informing them of her concerns. Disappointingly, she received no response from the Church's Moderator, Thomas Murray, or Clerk of Session, Dr Ian Brown, or many other senior ministers in the Free Presbyterian Church such as John Greer, and the conference went ahead as planned. The student was aware that such sharing of a platform would have been unheard of in days gone by. She persisted in her inquiry but there was never any response from those mentioned above.

I raise this here because one of the two men contacted was Dr Ian Brown, current minister of the Martyrs Memorial Free Presbyterian Church and Clerk of the Free Presbyterian Church of Ulster. Brown, who fills the pulpit of the late Dr Ian Paisley, is renowned for his recent project *The Reformation Room*.[93] This project involves a room at the Martyrs Memorial Church which showcases the life of the Reformers and offers tours throughout the year. Brown, it appears, has great interest in commemorating the Reformers. It is alarming, however, that he did not even respond to concerns regarding what appeared to be a modern-day compromise of the very truth the Reformers stood for.

Martin Luther's entire life was characterised by a sincerity of spirit; this even secular biographers acknowledge. Ronald Bainton pinpoints the effectiveness of Luther's stand when he contrasts the Reformer with the popes of the Renaissance, whom he describes as "secularised, flippant, frivolous, sensual, magnificent and unscrupulous."[94] Luther, by contrast, was meticulously sincere, and, when laid hold of by God, this solitary figure was used to revive the church in Europe and restore Christianity to its rightful place in society. Following Luther's stand, as Bainton notes, "men [once again] cared enough for the faith to die for it."[95]

Luther's spirit is a sharp contrast to the opportunistic spirit of the ministers of today, who embalm his tomb but share not his conviction for the truth. Luther did not embrace and promote religiosity: rather, his religious convictions were so sincere that he attacked his own church in the selling of indulgences. For Luther, religion, not religiosity, was paramount: Bainton summarizes this central tenet of his beliefs with eloquence: "These were Luther's religious principles: that religion is paramount, ... all institutions must accord to religion the right of way...all human relations must be conditioned by it...secure only if grounded in a common faith."[96] The ministers of our day claim to commemorate the Reformation: yet many deny by their lives and actions Luther's principle that doctrine should condition human relations, and instead join hands with those who fellowship with ecumenists.

It has been said of Luther that his contemporaries were sometimes "appalled that he would disrupt human relations or churchly unities over a single point of doctrine."[97] What a burning and shining light, what an example to follow; "to the law and to the testimony" was his guiding principle (Isa. 8:20). How sad today to hear of commemorative organisations composed of so-called fundamentalists and Jesuit priests, good wishes being expressed to centres of ecumenism, and Free Presbyterian ministers in conversation with Roman Catholic priests. How different to the Luther of the 16th century who believed that "to deny God in one point is to attack God in all."[98] How desparate the need to realise that perhaps those first to commemorate Luther would be also quickest to resist the *true* spirit in which Luther lived and expended his every breath.

We witness in the church today the *confluence* of holy doctrine and unholy living in churches once known for their allegiance to a pure gospel. Free Presbyterians are on the dance floor, and loose living and fornication is widespread in professedly fundamentalist churches. Ministers duplicitously exercise a benevolent attitude towards the sins of the age and yet profess uncompromising allegiance to the historic doctrines of the faith. They may fool men, but they do not fool God. On this the 500th anniversary of Luther's principled stand at Wittenberg, it is all good and well to set up Reformation memorials and museums and distribute commemorative literature. If, however, we turn a blind eye to sin and immorality in the church, we are ourselves taking the first step on the road to idolatry. Those who

> We witness in the church today the confluence of holy doctrine and unholy living in churches once known for their allegiance to a pure gospel.

adopt such an approach have become the dumb dogs of which Isaiah spoke (Isa. 56:10) and the hypocrites which our Lord berated (Mt. 23:29-33).

A true allegiance to the truth is one which is sincere. The word sincere comes from the Latin words *sine cera* or "without wax": the term was used to distinguish the work of skilled Roman sculptors from the imposters who used wax to hide the imperfections in their work. We witness today profuse religious profession with a "waxing over" of blatant refusal to adhere to God's standard of holiness. A profession of allegiance to the doctrines of the Bible, however, must be backed up by an equal concern for the personal holiness and practical purity of the church. Otherwise, such professions of orthodoxy cannot be judged sincere. I challenge Free Presbyterians and all Christians of our day to confront the evils that are insidiously destroying the church from within. Only by doing this can our lauding of Martin Luther be judged sincere.

Ultimately, ministers are approved in addressing the ills of their own day and not hiding behind the work of Martin Luther or other saints mightily used of God. It is sad today to see fornicators and adulterers called on to the church pulpit to minister in song. Many churches today profess loudly the doctrines of the Reformation, yet turn a blind eye to the sin and immorality in the midst. Unless there is evidenced interest to deal with and speak out against today's brazen sin that is destroying the church before our eyes, then "building of the tombs" is of no consequence (Mt. 23:29). The banner and heritage we stand under counts for nothing if by our actions we show our faith to be counterfeit.

The following quote has been attributed to Luther (although this has never been proven):

> If I profess, with the loudest voice and the clearest exposition, every portion of the truth of God except precisely that little point which the world and the devil are at that moment attacking, I am not confessing Christ, however boldly I may be professing Christianity. Where the battle rages the loyalty of the soldier is proved; and to be steady on all the battlefield besides is mere flight and disgrace to him if he flinches at that one point.

A true allegiance to the truth is one which is sincere.

Martin Luther is said to have warned his flock that "even if they were publicly open about just about every other aspect of their Christian faith, but chose to not admit their belief on some single point of doctrine (for fear of what might happen to them if their conviction on that one point became known) they were effectively denying Christ, period."[99] His grand objective was to encourage his followers to speak out and speak up even when faced with terrible opposition. For Luther, justification was the *articulus stantis et cadentis ecclesiae* of his day (the article by which the church stood or fell). Today seminars, books, and even museums vociferously proclaiming justification by faith alone abound, but there is a great wind of compromise on facing the equally pressing evils of our day: worldliness and immorality in the pew, and ecumenism and formalism in the pulpit.

At this the 500th anniversary of the Reformation, let us view with a measure of suspicion the widespread practice of visiting Luther's town of Wittenberg and posing by the statues of the Reformers. It was Luther himself who declared that "The true Christian pilgrimage is not to Rome, or Jerusalem, but to the prophets, the Psalms, and the Gospels."[100] Many now visiting the places where this man laboured, testified and preached have never made the only pilgrimage which Luther counted of true worth. The Scriptures alone, and nothing else, Bainton notes, was Luther's "great objective aid...because this is the written record of the revelation of God in Christ."[101] Luther, I believe, would be aghast at the calibre of many self-professed ministers who are claiming an interest in his cause by taking cruises and trips to the lands of the Reformation. Luther came to loathe the pilgrimage, which he himself had engaged in, as supplanting the only true journey of the saved soul: "Diligently read the Psalms, prophets, gospels...[for] rather than walk about holy places we can thus pause at our thoughts, examine our hearts, and visit the real promised land and paradise of eternal life."[102]

95

The Pied Piper

Thank God for Martin Luther, and the legacy of his life. Thank God for the Reformation of the 16th century. May God give us those in this day who truly follow Luther's example. It is now that matters, it is the present that counts. Needed in the pulpit are men who love the truth and prove it by their lives and actions!

Whenever the Church has been thoroughly distinct from the world she has always prospered.

Charles Haddon Spurgeon

6 | A Call to Action

Who is on the LORD's side?

Exodus 32:26

The enterprise *Embrace Socials* has been active in providing party entertainment in Northern Ireland since the early 2000s. Styling itself as "Northern Ireland's Premier Christian Entertainment Providers," *Embrace Socials* claims to be "Northern Ireland's Busiest Christian Group."[103] This enterprise has close links with all major evangelical denominations in Northern Ireland, including Free Presbyterians. Its primary business is to arrange parties and dances, as well as "worship events", at venues across Northern Ireland; it regularly runs events in Presbyterian and Methodist church halls, as well as at secular venues.

One of *Embrace Socials* main goals at the functions it arranges is to get everybody out on the dance floor. Its homepage features the verse Romans 5:8 in the King James Version of the Bible juxtaposed alongside a screen bearing the name of the song "Long Way to Tipperary." The former is a popular music hall dance tune which was penned in a Warwickshire pub in the early 1900s;[104] it was written to express the pining of the Irish abroad for the family they had left behind – Tipperary being a county in the South-West of Ireland. Despite the historic opposition of the church to social dancing, *Embrace Socials* by its very name encourages the dance and exhorts all to embrace (which means "willingly accept or support") it.

> One of Embrace Socials' main goals, as its name suggests, is to get the Christian onto the dance floor.

Spiritual compromise never uplifts or ennobles but rather condemns and damns. A recent event conducted by Embrace Socials in conjunction with the University of Coleraine Christian Union appeared to show a cross-dresser taking part in the festivities and receiving the "best group" prize for fancy dress with his teammates. Surely, the curse of God will fall upon those who would take the holy things of His Word and His Name and profane by using them in causes and places where He is not (1 Sam. 4:3).

The Church on the Dance Floor

In participating in *Embrace Socials*, Christians are sadly drinking from a poisoned chalice, and indicating how far they have fallen from their first love. It is sad to see prominent Free Presbyterian ministers sitting watching their congregations on the dance floor jiving the night away, with worldly music blaring. These things ought not to be. It is an offence to a holy God. The English "Prince of Preachers" Charles Spurgeon declared regarding the social dance: "However pleasing the dances of Herodias may have been to Herod, they were death to John the Baptist. The caperings and wantonings of the ball-room are death to the solemn influences of the ministry, and many an ill-ended life first received its bent for evil amid the flippancies of gay assemblies met to trip away the hours."[105]

Embrace Socials' website confirms that they are "providers of traditional social & ceildh games and all the line dances in between."[106]   It is significant that the céilí was and is a major part of pagan Irish culture, dating back to pre-Famine times when social dancing at the crossroads would take place on Sunday evenings.[107] It was instrumental in the deanglicisation of Ireland and was pursued by the Gaelic League and the GAA to that end (the Gaelic League organised their first céilí in 1897).

There are two passages in Scripture that are of great significance when considering the dance. Exodus 32 records how certain of the Israelites, having been mightily delivered from Egypt, engaged in idolatry and immorality as they waited for Moses to come down from Mt. Sinai (Ex. 32:6). Here we note the joining in hand of idolatry and immorality, two practices which we are

101

warned in Scripture to flee (1 Cor. 6:18; 1 Cor. 10:14). The dancing of the Israelites at this junction was emblematic of their rebellion against God and his servant Moses (Ex. 32:23). The raucous revelry of the people was accompanied by lewd behaviour, and the people danced in the shadow of the calf which they had made. When Moses came down from the mount, he "saw the calf, and the dancing" (Ex. 32:19). This holy man adjudged their behaviour a "great sin" (Ex. 32:21) and a swift and terrible punishment was inflicted upon them.

Another passage in Scripture which is equally damning of the dance is Mark 6:14-29, which records the circumstances surrounding the execution of John the Baptist by Herod. Herod was clearly moved by the testimony of John the Baptist: Scripture declares that he "feared" John, considered him a man of good character, and enjoyed listening to him speak (Mk. 6:20). The dancing of the daughter of the adulterous Herodias, however, so moved Herod that he acceded to her request for the "head of John the Baptist" (Mk. 6:24). If any scene in Scripture illustrates the confluence of the dance with a loose tongue, adultery, and murder, surely it is this scene. One dance was what led to Herod's execution of a man whom the Lord Jesus Christ commended as the greatest of prophets (Mt. 11:11).

> The dancing of the Israelites at Mt. Sinai was emblematic of their rebellion against God and his servant Moses.

In the passage in Exodus 32, the judgment exacted on those who had engaged in the dance resulted in three thousand deaths (Ex. 32:28). Moses

102

declared, "Who is on the LORD's side?" (Ex. 32:26) and the Levites responded to his call. Their impartiality in executing the judgment of God at this point is later alluded to in Deuteronomy 33:9 and echoes the severe test of Deuteronomy 13 in dealing with the false prophet in the midst. Moses commanded the Levites to "slay every man his brother, and every man his companion, and every man his neighbour" (32:27). The Levites delivered a complete

> Levi's full obedience marks out the path for all those who would follow God in times of declension: immediate, wholehearted obedience devoid of sentimentality.

and objective implementation of God's judgment on sin. Levi's full obedience marks out the path for all those who would follow God in times of declension: immediate, wholehearted obedience devoid of sentimentality.

The question now remains: where are the Levites of today? The embrace of the social dance by those formerly marked for their separation from worldliness is indicative of a great decline in the spiritual temperature of the church in Northern Ireland. Where are those who will shoulder the responsibility of separating from and declaring against all that is grossly dishonouring to God? The call of Moses goes out again today, in conditions little different from those at Mt. Sinai: "Who is on the LORD's side?"

Power is Proportionate to Consecration

In the last 10 years, the scene in the church in Northern Ireland has changed rapidly. John Piper and other New Calvinist writers' books are now carried en masse by the Christian bookseller The FM (Faith Mission), which has bookshops in all major Protestant urban centres in the North and holds a near monopoly on the high street Christian book market. The decline in spirituality and practical Christian holiness evident from the examples just given cannot be considered in a vacuum: the popularity of John Piper's theology has doubtless had an influence. Tragically, there has been very few voices, if any, in the leadership of churches in Northern Ireland who have published or publicly warned against the heresy in Piper's teaching.

The age in which we now live is one in which there is little power evident in the church to judge sin. Evil, thus, remains largely unchallenged and heresy entrenches itself in places once renowned for fidelity and truth. Evil is unjudged, and the few who depart from it have become conspicuous by their stand (Isa. 59:15). The powerful exhortations to holiness of life and commitment to the service of God that once rang from so many pulpits are no more, and the same pulpits are occupied with men-pleasers with messages bereft of holy authority and lacking in heavenly zeal.

> The age in which we now live is one in which there is little power evident in the church to judge sin.

The power of holiness of life has long been discounted in Christian circles today; yet, it is inextricably linked with the ability to do combat with the powers of evil. As a result, evil triumphs on every hand. It was C.H. Spurgeon who, commentating on the life of Samson declared, "My first point shall be the strength of the consecrated, for they are strong men...Do you know that the strongest man in all the world is a consecrated man?"[108] Spurgeon, himself used mightily of God against the evils of his day, knew the secret of enduring power. He saw in the witnesses of Hebrews 11:35-37, those cruelly mocked, stoned, and sawn asunder, indestructible power born of consecration. These were men and women willing to pay the price of consecration, and heirs of its power.

Where are the men today who will "earnestly contend for the faith once delivered to the saints" and consecrate themselves to a worthy cause? Where are those who will judge the sin that

> "The strongest man in all the world is a consecrated man."

is "local" to them and to their church? Where are those who will employ all the God ordained exercises of church discipline against those who sin with impunity? Has such discipline a place in your church, and is the process which God has ordained initiated against those who offend against God?

It is the duty of pastors to discipline those within the church who persist in sin (1 Cor. 5:11-13), excommunicating offenders if necessary. Many today make a "protest" against evil, as Eli did, when he declared concerning the evil of his sons "it is no good report that I hear" (1 Sam. 2:24). His mild rebuke was no substitute for the decisive action against evil which God's law mandated him to take. Eli was but satisfying his own conscience by a half-hearted attempt at duty, when a full response was called for. His demurring mirrors that of Samson's parents, who proffered a similar rebuke to their erring son: "Is there never a woman among the daughters of thy brethren, or among all my people, that thou goest to take a wife of the uncircumcised Philistines?" (Judg. 14:3). In both cases, the rebuke was powerless, and the judgment of God followed.

Investigating Error and Dealing with Heresy

The Old Testament lays down clear expectations about the spirit of jealousy for the truth which God expected of the people of Israel. Deuteronomy 13 dealt clearly with the scenario of a false teacher, or a "dreamer of dreams", arising to entice the people to "go after other gods, which thou hast not known, and let us serve them" (Deut. 13:2).

> The people were not only to passively refuse to yield to the false prophet's exhortation, but to actively prosecute him.

The people were not only to passively refuse to yield to such an exhortation, they were also to actively prosecute the false prophet, and to implement the death penalty (Deut. 13:5). The sentiment of this passage, albeit not its penalties, are echoed in the fervour of Paul's exhortation in Galatians 1:8: "But though we, or an angel from heaven, preach any other gospel unto you than that which we have preached unto you, let him be accursed." Even should the false prophet be a close family member, God clearly exhorted:

"thou shalt surely kill him; thine hand shall be first upon him to put him to death" (Deut. 13:9).

The reason for the rise of heresy is not necessarily the withdrawal of God from the church but His *proving* of it. Of the false prophet in Israel, God declared, "for the LORD your God proveth you, to know whether ye love the LORD your God with all your heart and with all your soul" (Deut. 13:3). The presence and activity of a false prophet was intended to provoke the true Israelite to a fervent investigation and opposition of the same: "inquire, and make search, and ask diligently; and, behold, if it be truth, and the thing certain..." (Deut. 13:14). So today, no less impassioned a response is anticipated by God's elect: when heresy arises, and new gods are chosen (Judg. 5:8), the church must apply herself to finding out the truth, without prejudice or partiality: "There must be also heresies among you, that they which are approved may be made manifest among you" (1 Cor. 11:19). It is the duty of the church to judge those that are within (1 Cor. 5:12,13), when the false teacher encourages us to shake off restraint and serve gods that will not only countenance but encourage our immoralities.

Returning to the Authority of the Scriptures

One of the greatest blessings of the Reformation was the open Bible. The reading of the Scriptures in the vernacular, popularised by the technology of mechanical movable type in the printing press, turned Europe upside down in the days of the Protestant Reformation. Before the start of the 16th century, spiritual darkness covered Europe and the doctrines of the Gospel lay buried beneath a mass of man-made traditions: indulgences and penance, pilgrimages, worship of the saints and the "Virgin Mary", and their relics. With the opening of the Scriptures came the enlightening of the mind, as distinct from the merely sentimental impact of images and idolatry. For the first time, hundreds upon thousands tasted the truth for themselves, in their own language, and Protestantism became entrenched where the Bible was read. The hand of God worked mightily, and this work would not be overthrown, for many had found liberty from the bondage of Romanism. God's "rule of law" was laid bare, in all its unchanging permanence.

Let us hearken to Luther's words as we celebrate the 500th anniversary of the Reformation: "putting aside all human writings we should spend all the more persistent labour on Holy Scriptures alone."[109] A return to the final and only infallible authority of the Scripture is imperative if the church is to recover its power in

> Luther contrasted the pursuit of human writings and human authors with an acquaintance with the Word of God itself.

these "perilous times" (2 Tim. 3:1). Critically, Luther contrasted the pursuit of human writings and human authors with an acquaintance with the Word of God itself. The blind allegiance to pastors and leaders rife in the church today is a gross sin. Rather, the first principles for every believer ought to be those found in the Word of God, and all conclusions of men which do not agree with Scripture should be rejected. Scripture alone must remain the judge of all men, the test of all doctrines, and the master of all books.

The health of the church is to be assessed by the ordinary Christian's ability to measure all things by "the law and the testimony" (Isa. 8:20). Indeed, the New Testament saints were commended for doing this to even the words of the apostles (Acts 17:11; 1 Cor. 10:15). When the church is no longer holy and consecrated, but joins the world in its revelry on the dance floor, the nobility of individual obedience remains the lifeline for its survival which God has employed again and again. Then is the time to take the side of God against the uncleanness of the age: "come out from among them, and be ye separate, saith the Lord, and touch not the unclean thing; and I will receive you, and will be a Father unto you, and ye shall be my sons and daughters" (2 Cor. 6:17-18).

Cultivating Directness in an Age of Apostasy

When God has worked in revival, it has always been to call the people of God back to old truths, former obedience, and faithful precepts: "Stand ye in the ways, and see, and ask for the old paths, where is the good way, and walk therein, and ye shall find rest for your souls" (Jer. 6:16). God does not contradict Himself or require different obedience of different generations (Numbers 23:19). Today the church, as in every age, must make a choice: the world or the cross, falsehood or truth, Piper or Christ. Those who make the choice to serve Christ must be willing to bear His Name and His truth before a world that hates Him as much as it ever did (John 17:14).

John Piper is not a preacher of the Gospel, but a heretic. He is a false prophet who is leading multitudes of young people to believe that devotion to Christ is compatible with sensuality, worldliness, and pseudo-intellectual vanity. May God give us once again the directness of the Apostles. Peter prophesied that the false prophets of the Old Testament dispensation would be supplanted by false teachers in the New Testament dispensation. He called their heresies "damnable". He knew their "feigned words" would make merchandise of the Church, but he remained assured that God would judge them and that their demise and damnation was imminent (2 Pet. 2:3).

Christ warned against false prophets in one of the first sermons He ever preached: "Beware of false prophets, which come to you in sheep's clothing, but inwardly they are ravening wolves. Ye shall know them by their fruits" (Mt. 7:15-16). We are commanded to examine the fruit of those who teach, for Christ warned in the same chapter that "not every one that saith unto me, Lord, Lord, shall enter into the kingdom of heaven; but he that doeth the will of my Father which is in heaven" (Mt. 7:21). Our examination of John Piper has proven that his ministry does not promote obedience to Christ's commands. Rather, "unclean" (2 Pet. 2:10) could be written over the whole of the New Calvinist movement and the influence of John Piper. Piper has brought sensuality into the pulpit; it is little wonder that it is now rife in the pews.

> Piper has brought sensuality into the pulpit; it is little wonder that it is now rife in the pews.

110

What is the Christian's duty?

The duty of the Christian is to actively oppose the work of the devil when and where he meets it. What good are the injunctions of the writers in 2 Peter and Jude if they leave us with none of the "Thus saith the Lord" clarity of the Old Testament prophets? How relevant is God's truth to our time, if we are restricted from naming and resisting the false teachers of our day? New Calvinism's foray into the church is an evil work, detracting from the historic truths of the Christian faith while feigning a revival of interest in them.

Like all the devil's works, New Calvinism's influence is subtle, and this explains its remarkable success in what once were faithful churches and impregnable bulwarks of old-time Christianity. New Calvinists rarely frame their arguments in terms of what they are against. They do not openly declare their disagreement with and opposition towards keeping the Sabbath day, chastity in conversation, separation from ecumenism, and Christian distinctiveness from the world. Instead they seek to undermine all these distinctives by a lop-sided message which beguiles unstable and restless souls and pollutes lives with a cheap grace.

> New Calvinism's foray into the church is an evil work, detracting from the historic truths of the Christian faith while feigning a revival of interest in them.

The only way in which Christians can alert the church to the errors of this movement and

111

deliver their own souls is to inform God's people of the darker side of New Calvinism. Those who follow and propagate the teachings of John Piper and other New Calvinists should be challenged as to their allegiance to the commands of Christ and to the error of their ways. Those who find a proclivity to the antinomianism of the New Calvinist movement in their pastor should seek a church where the gospel in its purity will be preached and the law of God exalted as a guide to the saints. Many pastors who profess fundamentalism are now exalting New Calvinism. I would encourage you to come out of those places, regardless of the denomination: "come out from among them and be ye separate" (2 Cor. 6:17). Young people should be counselled that the worldly Christianity of Piper and other New Calvinists is a sugar-coated lie which destroys the witness of the Christian and ends in the departure of the presence and blessing of God.

> New Calvinism's doctrines on sanctification are as opposed to God's truth as Rome's doctrine on justification, and just as serious to the welfare of God's people.

New Calvinism is as opposed to the true biblical gospel as Rome was in the 16th century. It was only when Luther opposed Rome with his publication of the 95 Theses in 1517, however, that God worked through him to revive the elect of God. The papal bull which the pope and his allies dispatched was then no match for this man of God, who shook Europe with his proclamation of God's truth that "the just shall live by faith."

New Calvinism's doctrines on sanctification are as opposed to God's truth as Rome's doctrine on justification, and just as serious to the welfare of God's people. Let us rise to the challenge in these "perilous times" (2 Tim. 3:1) and be the remnant who will honour God's Word and champion His cause. The day is indeed dark, but God's truth is a light which pierces the darkness.

Let us take courage that when His light shines in the darkness, the darkness cannot overcome it (Jn. 1:5).

The triumph of John Piper and other false teachers on the ruins of an unholy and ineffective church arises in a vacuum: a vacuum of faithful minsters able and determined to teach the church (2 Tim. 2:2).

I would encourage you to rise up and speak out:

When men supplant the sacred page,

With errors from a darkened age,

And with God's truth a warfare wage—

Speak out!

When men feel not affliction's rod,

And shun the path their fathers trod,

And cast aside their faith in God—

Speak out![110]

Despite this dark and evil day, this generation must faithfully pass on God's unchanging truth to the next. So, as Nehemiah of old, I would exhort you, *fight*, fight not for yourselves alone, but for the next generation. May their spiritual welfare, and the promise of God to multiply your efforts, motivate you to service in this holy war:

> Be not ye afraid of them: remember the LORD, which is great and terrible, and fight for your brethren, your sons and your daughters, your wives, and your houses. (Neh. 4:14).

Acknowledgements

This book would not have been possible without the selfless dedication of many who worked behind the scenes. At the top of the list would undoubtedly be my mother, Martina Burke. Her belief in the necessity of this book inspired me to commence it in late 2017, and her passion for the relevance and importance of its message never waned. She also served as the primary editor of The Pied Piper, making literally dozens of helpful suggestions. Thank you for putting the pen in my hand as a child, and for your spiritual wisdom over the years. I owe you so much (Phil. 1:19).

Thank you also to Josiah Burke for designing the book cover, and to others who assisted greatly in the collating of many primary sources for the information found in this book, as well as helping to proofread the final editions.

To my father Seán Burke and others in my local church who prayed for and encouraged me as I wrote this book, I extend my sincere thanks, and ask for your continued prayers for its wide circulation.

Contact

If you would like the author to speak at your church, or wish to order further copies of this book, you can get in touch by email: info@thepiedpiperbook.com

Please include your name and address with all queries. Queries and orders can also be made online via the website http://www.thepiedpiperbook.com.

Index

fundamentalism 4, 10, 11, 28, 29, 92, 112, 125
neo-evangelicalism 12, 23, 28, 29, 30, 86
New Calvinism iii, 4, 5, 7, 9, 12, 15, 18, 44, 50, 54, 64, 66, 111, 112, 113, 133
Reformation, the 9, 15, 44, 45, 48, 73, 80, 88, 89, 90, 91, 92, 93, 94, 95, 96, 107, 108, 135, 136
Roman Catholicism 3, 11, 12, 23, 32, 40, 44, 47, 48, 49, 51, 79, 88, 90, 92, 130, 131
Cranmer, Thomas 1

D

Desiring God Ministries 8, 9, 30, 32, 40, 46, 49, 66, 73, 88, 125, 126, 127, 132, 135
Driscoll, Mark 46, 64, 72, 73, 133, 134

E

Embrace Socials 96, 99, 100, 101, 137

F

Faith Mission, the 104
Foxe, John 27, 125, 127
Free Presbyterian Church, the 86, 87, 88, 89, 90, 91, 92, 101
Fuller, Daniel 23, 29, 30, 47, 130

G

Giglio, Louie 32, 125
Graham, Billy 10, 11, 12, 28, 29, 33, 49, 125, 126, 131
Green, Brian 86, 135
Greer, John 89, 90
Grey, Jane 27

H

Hamilton, Patrick 27
Henry, Matthew 60, 61, 67, 85, 132, 133, 135
Hooper, John 27

Endnotes

Introduction

1   See John Foxe, Foxe's Book of Martyrs, accessed 25 November 2017, p.169, at http://kotisatama.net/files/kotisatama/ Tekstit_ja_kirjat/foxe.pdf.

Chapter 1: Why John Piper?

2   See David Mathis "Who is John Piper?" in For the Fame of God's Name: Essays in Honour of John Piper (Wheaton, IL: Crossway, 2010), p. 37.

3   John Piper has spoken at the Passion Conference organised by his friend, Louie Giglio, at least 16 times. He first spoke at a Passion Conference in 1997. John Piper's speaking at the Third Lausanne Congress on World Evangelisation in Cape Town, South Africa is made available by the Lausanne Movement at https:// www.youtube.com/watch?v=Guct72gPSX0.

4   See Mathis "Who is John Piper?", p. 38.

5   Justin Taylor mentions this in his dissertation "John Piper: The Making of a Christian Hedonist" (Southern Baptist Theological Seminary, 2015), p. 16. A more detailed analysis of Bill Piper's beliefs is found on the Desiring God website, in a 2008 message delivered by John Piper. See https://www.desiringgod. org/messages/evangelist-bill-piper-fundamentalist-full-of-grace- and-joy.

6   See the book by Curtis Mitchell, God in the Garden: The Story of the Billy Graham New York Crusade (Garden City, NY:

Doubleday, 1957), book cover. Also available at http://www.ccel. us/garden.toc.html.

7   See William Martin, "Evangelicalism: Billy Graham", accessed 25 November 2017 at http://www.christianitytoday.com/ history/issues/issue-65/evangelicalism-billy-graham.html.

8   Ibid.

9   See Jon M. Graham, "Billy Graham and the Catholics", The Huffington Post, 4 November 2014, accessed 25 November 2017 at https://www.huffingtonpost.com/jon-m-sweeney/billy-graham-catholics-_b_6100092.html

10   See the article, accessed 25 November 2017, at https:// www.gotquestions.org/heresy-definition.html for this quote and a definition of heresy.

11   See the dictionary entry on the online Merriam Webster Dictionary at https://www.merriam-webster.com/ dictionary/heresy.

12   Justin Taylor, "John Piper: The Making of a Christian Hedonist", p. 14.

13   See King James Bible Word Book entry for the definition of this word (Nashville: Thomas Nelson, 2002).

Chapter 2: The Real John Piper

14   John Piper, Desiring God: Meditations of a Christian Hedonist (Colorado Springs: Multnomah, 2011), p.10.

15   James B. Ramsey, Revelation: An Exposition of the First 11 Chapters (Carlisle, PA: Banner of Truth, 1977), p. 156.

16   See John Piper's sermon at Passion 2017, in which he declares that "Disobedience — or law-breaking — is not the ultimate essence of evil". John Piper, "The Ultimate Essence of Evil", 3 January 2017, accessed 27 November 2017, https://www. desiringgod.org/messages/the-ultimate-essence-of-evil.

17   John Foxe, Foxe's Book of Martyrs, accessed 25 November 2017, p.155, at http://kotisatama.net/files/kotisatama/Tekstit_ja_ kirjat/foxe.pdf.

18   See Rose French, "Key Minnesota Pastors Opt Out of Marriage Fight', 2 September 2012, accessed 25 November 2017, http://www.startribune.com/key-minnesota-pastors-opt-out-of-marriage-fight/159819565/. John Piper stated in a sermon before the vote "Don't press the organization of the church or her pastors into political activism." See Jonathan Parnell, 'Your Pastor Is Not Your Political Activist', 24 June 2012, accessed 25 November 2017, https://www.desiringgod.org/articles/your-pastor-is-not-your-political-activist.

19   See Harold J. Ockenga's Foreword to Harold Lindsell, The Battle for the Bible (Grand Rapids, MI: Zondervan, 1976), p. 11.

20   See Justin Taylor, John Piper: Making of a Christian Hedonist, p. 23.

21   Piper, Desiring God, p. 13.

22   See Piper, "20 Reasons I Don't Take Potshots at Fundamentalists", 2 June 2008, accessed 25 November 2017, https:// www.desiringgod.org/articles/20-reasons-i-dont-take-potshots-at-fundamentalists . Another article published by Piper is entitled "Praise God for Fundamentalists", 31 October 2007, accessed 25 November 2017, https://www.desiringgod.org/articles/praise-

god-for-fundamentalists.

23   See the video at John Piper, "A Christmas Greeting and Poem", 25 December 2009, accessed 25 November 2017, https://www.desiringgod.org/articles/a-christmas-greeting-and-poem.

24   See Talitha Piper's blogpost "Twenty Two [Things]", 12 October 2017, accessed 25 November 2017, https://talitharuth.wordpress.com/2017/10/12/twenty-two-things/ .

25   This article was originally published in the Decision magazine and later republished in different outlets. See Abraham Piper, "Let Them Come Home", 28 August 2007, accessed 25 November 2017, https://billygraham.org/decision-magazine/september-2007/let-them-come-home/.

26   Ibid.

27   See CNBC interview by Catherine Clifford, "This dad used to be a forklift driver—now his blog brings in $17 million a year", 18 August 2017, accessed 25 November 2017, https://www.cnbc.com/2017/08/17/22-words-started-as-this-dads-blog-now-it-makes-17-million-a-year.html.

28   Twenty Two Words, "Jesus Takes the Ice Bucket Challenge", 20 August 2014, accessed 25 November 2017, https://www.youtube.com/watch?v=gXcptsz5j4k

29   See David C. Cook, "On Choosing a Tattoo – Barnabas Piper", 29 June 2015, accessed 25 November 2017, https://www.youtube.com/watch?v=l7IcTi1KQ3Q

30   See Barnabas Piper, "When A Marriage Dies", 10 January 2017, accessed 25 November 2017, a cached copy available at https://

web.archive.org/web/20170111131845/https://barnabaspiper.
com/2017/01/when-a-marriage-dies.html.

31   See Joshua Pease, "Barnabas Piper on Divorce—The
Scarlet Letter of the Evangelical World", 7 June 2017, accessed
25 November 2017,   https://churchleaders.com/pastors/304824-
barnabas-piper-divorce-scarlet-letter-evangelical-world.html.

32   See Barnabas Piper's biographical entry, where he
provides links for "booking or scheduling information": https://
barnabaspiper.com/about.

33   Charles Bridges, Proverbs (Carlisle, PA: Banner of Truth,
1994), p. 186.

Chapter 3: The Doctrine of John Piper

34   See Alexa, the internet information company, which
contains listings of the most popular websites on the internet. As
of the end of November 2017, Piper's website ranked number 10 in
Alexa's "Christianity" list, even when websites of the major cults,
such as Mormons and Jehovah's Witnesses, are included.

35   John Piper, "Has My Sexual Sin Made Me Unsavable?",
29 February 2016, accessed 25 November 2017, Audio Transcript
of Interview,   https://www.desiringgod.org/interviews/has-my-
sexual-sin-made-me-unsavable.

36   John Piper, "John Piper Interviews Rick Warren on
Doctrine", 27 May 2011, accessed 25 November 2017, https://www.
desiringgod.org/articles/john-piper-interviews-rick-warren-on-
doctrine.

37   Kathy Schiffer, "Megachurch Pastor Rick Warren Joins

Pope Francis in Support of Common Mission", 19 December 2014, accessed 25 November 2017, https://aleteia.org/2014/12/19/megachurch-pastor-rick-warren-joins-pope-francis-in-support-of-common-mission/.

38   See Rick Warren's interview with Raymond Arroyo of World Over on 20 November 2014, accessed 25 November 2017, available at https://www.youtube.com/watch?v=Pzw8rzldRMs.

39   See especially John W. Robbins, "Pied Piper", The Trinity Review (June 2002), p.7, this article, accessed 27 November 2017, available at http://www.trinityfoundation.org/PDF/The%20Trinity%20Review%200197a%20PiedPiper.pdf.

40   Daniel Fuller,   The Unity of the Bible (Grand Rapids, MI: Zondervan, 1992), p. 272, as quoted in John Piper, Future Grace (Sisters, Oregon: Multnomah, 1995), p. 206.

41   See John Robbins, "Pied Piper", p.7.

42   See John Robbins, "Pied Piper", p.1.

43   John Piper, "Don't Play the Lottery for Me!", 1 January 2003, accessed 27 November 2017, https://www.desiringgod.org/articles/dont-play-the-lottery-for-me.

44   John Piper, "The Spirit of Joy", 3 March 1981, accessed 27 November 2017, https://www.desiringgod.org/articles/the-spirit-of-joy.

45   John Piper, "Clarifying My Words About Roman Catholic 'Heresy'", 14 March 2013, accessed 27 November 2017, https://www.desiringgod.org/articles/clarifying-my-words-about-roman-catholic-heresy

46   Foxe, Foxe's Book of Martyrs, p. 144.

47   John Piper, "If You Had Two Minutes to Talk With the Pope, What Would You Say to Him?", 15 December 2009, accessed 27 November 2017, https://www.desiringgod.org/interviews/if-you-had-two-minutes-to-talk-with-the-pope-what-would-you-say-to-him.

48   Piper, "Clarifying My Words About Roman Catholic 'Heresy'".

49   See Jon M. Graham, "Billy Graham and the Catholics".

50   Grant Wacker, America's Pastor (London: Belknap Press, 2014), p. 191.

51   First Things is the magazine of the Institute of Religion and Public Life, an ecumenical institute founded by Richard Neuhaus. "Evangelicals and Catholics Together" is another initiative of this Institute.

52   Logan Paul Gage, "Its Vespers Somewhere", 19 May 2015, book review accessed 27 November 2017, https://www.firstthings.com/web-exclusives/2015/05/its-vespers-somewhere.

53   All quotations in this paragraph taken from Arthur Pink, Gleanings in Exodus, as appeared in "Studies in the Scriptures", April 1926.

54   John Piper, "Are Christians Under the Ten Commandments?", 7 August 2010, accessed 27 November 2017, transcript of video interview, available at: https://www.desiringgod.org/interviews/are-christians-under-the-10-commandments.

55   Art Lindsley, "Moral Law and the Ten Commandments", 19 November 2013, accessed 27 November 2017, https://tifwe.org/resource/moral-law-and-the-ten-commandments/.

56   See the title and subtitle of the Timothy Keller's book The Prodigal God (London: Hodder & Stoughton, 2009).

57   Gil Kaufman, "Carrie Underwood Comes Out in Support of Same-Sex Marriage", 6 December 2012, accessed 27 November 2017, http://www.mtv.com/news/1687156/carrie-underwood-gay-marriage/.

58   See David F. Wells, cover quotation in For the Fame of God's Name: Essays in Honour of John Piper (Wheaton, IL: Crossway, 2010), p. 1.

59   See John MacArthur's words at the Desiring God 2007 National Conference in an interview between John Piper and MacArthur conducted by Justin Taylor. "A Conversation with John Piper and John MacArthur", 28 September 2007, accessed 17 November 2017, audio transcript at https://www.desiringgod.org/interviews/a-conversation-with-john-piper-and-john-macarthur.

60   See Arthur Pink, Gleanings in Exodus (Lafayette, IN: Sovereign Grace Publishers, 2002), p. 160.

Chapter 4: The Fruits of John Piper

61   The expositor Matthew Henry, commentary on 1 Cor. 6:12.

62   William Wilberforce was a convert of John Wesley. See Wesley's full letter at "Letter to William Wilberforce", 24 February 1791, accessed 27 November 2017, http://www.umcmission.org/Find-Resources/John-Wesley-Sermons/The-Wesleys-and-Their-Times/Letter-to-William-Wilberforce.

63   See commentary on Mt. 7:16, Jamieson, R., Fausset, A. R., & Brown, D, Commentary Critical and Explanatory on the Whole

Bible Vol. 2 (Oak Harbor, WA: Logos Research Systems, Inc., 1997), p.30.

64 David Van Biema, "Ten Ideas Changing the World Right Now: The New Calvinism", 12 March 2009, in Time Magazine, available at http://content.time.com/time/specials/packages/article/0,28804,1884779_1884782_1884760,00.html.

65 John Piper, "What Do You Think of Tattoos and Body-Piercing?", 29 August 2007, accessed 26 November 2017, audio resource available at https://www.desiringgod.org/interviews/what-do-you-think-of-tattoos-and-body-piercing.

66 See statements regarding tattoos made by Mark Driscoll's on 28 May 2006, available at http://truthwatchers.com/tattoos-biblical-view/.

67 Katherine Zappone, interview with Irish Media in early 2017.

68 In 2005, for example, John Piper edited and contributed to a whole book on the subject of sex, entitled Sex and the Supremacy of Christ (Wheaton, IL: Crossway, 2005).

69 Matthew Henry, commentary on Numbers 25, available at http://biblehub.com/commentaries/mhcw/numbers/25.htm.

70 Referenced here is the Carrie Underwood performance at Passion 2017. See chapter 3, section entitled "Can Hedonism Engender Holiness?"

71 James B. Ramsey, Revelation: An Exposition of the First 11 Chapters (Carlisle, PA: Banner of Truth, 1977), p. 154.

72 John Piper, "Gutsy Guilt", 19 October 2007, in Christianity Today: http://www.christianitytoday.com/ct/2007/october/38.72.

html.

73   John Piper, 10 September 1984, accessed 27 November 2017, https://www.desiringgod.org/articles/missions-and-masturbation

74   John Piper, message at Passion 2007 in Atlanta Georgia, available at https://www.desiringgod.org/messages/how-to-deal-with-the-guilt-of-sexual-failure-for-the-glory-of-christ-and-his-global-cause.

75   See the interview between CNN's Piers Morgan and Mark Driscoll, 10 March 2012: http://religion.blogs.cnn.com/2012/03/10/pastor-mark-driscoll-on-marriage-sex/.

76   See article by David Sessions, 12 January 2012, accessed 27 November 2017, https://www.thedailybeast.com/mark-driscolls-sex-manual-real-marriage-scandalizes-evangelicals.

77   John Piper, "Do You Regret Partnering with Mark Driscoll?", 13 November 2014, accessed 27 November 2017, audio transcript of interview: https://www.desiringgod.org/interviews/do-you-regret-partnering-with-mark-driscoll.

78   See French, "Key Minnesota Pastors Opt Out of Marriage Fight."

Chapter 5: Taking Back the Church

79   Ronald H. Bainton, Here I Stand: A Life of Martin Luther (Nashville, TN: Abingdon Press, 1950), p. 60.

80   See a copy of the text of a sermon by evangelist W. P. Nicholson, "The Perils of the Christian", accessed on 18 November 2017, http://www.sermonindex.net/modules/newbb/viewtopic.

php?topic_id=15498&forum=34.

81   Ibid.

82   Matthew Henry, commentary on 1 Corinthians 5:13.

83   Matthew Henry, commentary on 1 Corinthians 5:12.

84   James Ramsey, Revelation: An Exposition, p. 476.

85   See Brian Green, "Infiltration by the Church of Rome", 4 January 1998, accessed 27 November 2017, a cached copy of this address   available   at: http://webcache.googleusercontent.com/ search?q=cache:_PqH75W-22gJ:www.ianpaisley.org/lectures. asp%3Finfiltration.htm+&cd=1&hl=en&ct=clnk&gl=ie.

86   Henry Chu, "Ian Paisley dies at 88; Northern Ireland firebrand turned peacemaker", in Los Angeles Times, 12 September 2014, accessed 27 November 2017, http://www.latimes.com/ world/europe/la-fg-ian-paisley-dies-20140912-story.html.

87   John Piper's introduction to Joel Beeke at Desiring God Pastors Conference 2011, see https://www.youtube.com/ watch?v=EY6d6WjpvMc.

88   See https://www.refo500.com/en/, accessed 18th November 2017.

89   Bodar's speech, made in October 2010 at Refo500, is available in Dutch on his personal website. Antoine Bodar, "Back to the One Church: Reformation – Mistake or Progress", posted 30 October 2010, accessed 27 November 2017, http://www.antoinebodar.nl/ lezing/refo-500/.

90   See the keynote speakers at the conference on   John   Owen   listed   at   http://www.tua.nl/index.

php?paginaID=182&archief=agendastuk.

91   See press release of the Puritan Reformed Theological Seminary, 15 September 2017, accessed 27 November 2017, https://prts.edu/press-release-theological-university-apeldoorn-prts-forge-strategic-partnership-dual-doctoral-program/.

92   See the listing of contributors to the Reformation Heritage KJV Study Bible at https://kjvstudybible.org/contributors/.

93   See the website created for this project, which lists Ian Brown as one of the 3 coordinators: https://www.thereformationroom.com/.

94   Ronald H. Bainton, Here I Stand: A Life of Martin Luther (Nashville TN: Abingdon Press, 1978), p. 6.

95   Bainton, Here I Stand, p. 6

96   Bainton, Here I Stand, p. 225.

97   Bainton, Here I Stand, p. 225.

98   Bainton, Here I Stand, p. 225.

99   See Carl Wieland, "Where the battle rages – a case of misattribution", 4 February 2010, accessed 27 November 2017, https://creation.com/battle-quote-not-luther.

100   Luther, as quoted in Bainton, Here I Stand, p. 288.

101   Luther, as quoted in Bainton, Here I Stand, p. 288.

102   Luther, as quoted in Grace Tiffany, Love's Pilgrimage (Newark, NJ: University of Delaware Press, 2006), p.149.

Chapter 6: A Call to Action

103   See the website of this enterprise, accessed 27 November 2017, http://embracesocials.co.uk/.

104   See Antonia Bannister, "Iconic country pub where 'It's A Long Way to Tipperary' was written goes up for sale", 7 March 2016, accessed 27 November 2017, http://www.coventrytelegraph. net/news/local-news/iconic-country-pub-its-long-11003245.

105   Charles Spurgeon, as quoted by R. A. Adams, The Social Dance (Kansas City, 1921), p.29.

106   See Embrace Socials website page entitled "Socials & Ceildhs": http://embracesocials.co.uk/services/socials%20%26%20 ceildhs.html.

107   See "The History of Irish Dance", extract from Arthur Flynn, Irish Dance (Appletree Press, 1998), at http://www.irelandseye. com/dance.html.

108   See C. H. Spurgeon, "Samson Conquered", 21 November 1858, sermon available at http://www.biblebb.com/files/ spurgeon/0224.htm.

109   Martin Luther, as quoted in Greg Allison, Historical Theology: An Introduction to Christian Doctrine (Grand Rapids, MI: Zondervan, 2011), p. 88.

110   An old poem, author unknown.

 CPSIA information can be obtained
at www.ICGtesting.com
Printed in the USA
LVHW081432290920
667400LV00019B/3656